ENGAGING NINEVEH

A Conservative Church, a Baptist Preacher,
and a Newfound Heart for Muslims

Praise for *Engaging Nineveh*

God, in His providence and grace, is bringing the nations to America. Some people find this terribly threatening. Others rejoice because it presents unique opportunities for showing the love of Christ and sharing the good news of the gospel.

One is not surprised when those who live in a rural context are slower to embrace change. My grandparents were farmers, salt-of-the-earth people, and they were in church every time the doors were open. They were kind, hardworking, and loved the Lord, but they were very resistant to change. It was just the way they were. They were not atypical.

So to read a story of a rural church that moved from suspicion and fear to embracing and loving Muslim immigrants is surprising, remarkable and inspiring. And that is what this short work by Joshua Phillips is. *Engaging Nineveh* weaves together, in a beautiful tapestry, biblical truth with the story of a church that acted on that truth.

The results are what you would expect: lives transformed for the glory of King Jesus. However, the transformed lives you will read about are not just those of Muslims who have come to Christ. It is about a church that began to see the nations that are coming to America in a whole new light. They began to see it as a good thing and not a bad thing. They saw it as a God thing!

At Southeastern Baptist Theological Seminary, where Josh Phillips received two degrees (Master of Divinity and a Doctor of Ministry), we are fond of saying: Every professor a Great Commission professor, every classroom a Great Commission classroom, and every student a Great Commission student who will GO and build Great Commission churches. The Lord has brought great joy to my heart in watching one of our graduates do exactly this. This book will both convict and challenge your heart. It certainly did mine.

Danny Akin, President
Southeastern Baptist Theological Seminary

Demographers tell us that currently there are about forty-five million foreign-born residents in the United States — refugees, immigrants and international students. By 2065, projections call for that number to grow to seventy-eight million. And the fastest-growing religious affiliation among them is Muslim. By 2030, the Muslim population is projected to more than double in the United States.

To reach North America with the gospel, the church in America is going to have to launch an aggressive Great Commission initiative focused on reaching these people whom God has brought to this country. Josh Phillips is one young man who has responded to this need. He knows the need. He knows the people. Read his story in *Engaging Nineveh* and find yourself wanting and willing to follow his example.

Jim Shaddix, W.A. Criswell Professor of Expository Preaching
Southeastern Baptist Theological Seminary

ENGAGING NINEVEH

A Conservative Church, a Baptist Preacher,
and a Newfound Heart for Muslims

JOSH PHILLIPS

Engaging Nineveh:

A Conservative Church, a Baptist Preacher, and a Newfound Heart for Muslims

Copyright © 2022 Josh Phillips

Scripture taken from the New King James Version®. Copyright © 1982 by Thomas Nelson. Used by permission. All rights reserved.

ISBN 978-1-955295-16-1

Courier Publishing
100 Manly Street
Greenville, South Carolina 29601
CourierPublishing.com

PUBLISHED IN THE UNITED STATES OF AMERICA

Dedication

This book is dedicated to those who contributed to this beautiful story.

I would like to thank Nik and Ruth Ripken for inspiring me to seek Muslims in my community.

I would also like to thank Dr. Joel Rainey and his wonderful wife, Amy, for leading by example in ministering to Muslims in our early days.

To my wife, Jaclyn, and my parents, Harold and Corkie Phillips, thank you for supporting me in this journey.

I also wish to dedicate this book to all those at Pleasant View Baptist Church and Salaam Center Ministries who continue to partner sacrificially to serve Middle Eastern people for the gospel cause and the glory of God.

I would also like to thank the anonymous donor who made this book possible.

Table of Contents

Foreword   xi

Section 1

Chapter 1	Look Around	17
Chapter 2	Look at Recent Decades	23
Chapter 3	Look at the Giants	31

Section 2

Chapter 4	Look in Scripture	39
Chapter 5	Look at the Path to Water	47
Chapter 6	Look to Nineveh	55
Chapter 7	Look to the Unclean	63
Chapter 8	Look Beyond the Wall of Partition	73

Section 3

Chapter 9	Look to Apply	81
Chapter 10	Look at My Tribe	87
Chapter 11	Looking to Lead	91
Chapter 12	Look to the Future	101

Appendix   105
Notes   109

Foreword

Perhaps every new ministry and initiative starts with a good, hard look in the mirror. Josh Phillips reveals, in his engaging first book, how one can face their own racial chasm — not only seeing Muslims as people for whom Christ died, but journeying until the family of Ishmael become one's personal friends.

Ruth and I have known Josh, his wife, Jaclyn, and his former church in Maryland for almost a decade. In many ways, our journey to sub-Saharan Africa was an easier and quicker spiritual journey than it was for Dr. Phillips and what defines white, Christian culture in the United States. *Engaging Nineveh* sneaks up on its readers. It takes racism and whatever separates us from our neighbors (global and local) and wraps it in humor and storytelling in order to deliver a heartwarming pilgrimage toward Jesus. We all forget that Jesus was not Caucasian. Given the painful divisions found in modern-day USA and exported globally, it stretches our imagination to remember that the historical Jesus' DNA is closer to that of Middle Eastern origin — Jew and Muslim — than to the DNA of Josh and myself.

Someone asked Billy Graham years ago what the number one hindrance was to the kingdom of God internationally. His response, "Racism," was instantaneous. What has most often challenged our ministry and damaged our souls in serving thirty-five years internationally? It is the racism and tribalism found among the tribes of sub-Saharan Africa and the clans of Somalis in the Horn of Africa. Racism weaves itself inside Bosnians and Serbs, and then hides in nationalism until Isaac and Ishmael fight and then go their separate ways.

Then comes along Josh, Jaclyn, and their church. In the interest of full disclosure, we met him in a class we taught in North Carolina. Josh could have taken the information received in that master's level course and filed it away as a good, educational experience. Instead, he allowed it to break him, to rearrange his spiritual DNA. He began to see Muslims everywhere. He began to count them, research them, and look for them. He refused any longer to repeat the idiom, "A good Muslim is a dead Muslim." He refused to allow loving his church, loving his childhood neighbors, and loving Muslims to remain separate boxes. With wisdom found in godly parents, he disseminated his loving, broken heart through his family and to his church.

Josh's book is a pilgrimage of hope and love. He combines his storytelling ability, country-boy humor, and faith in Jesus to challenge his readers to travel down the same road, where faith and racism cannot co-inhabit the same heart. Josh says that if you believe something, you must do something. A change of heart results in a change of action. One of the strengths of this book is how he always takes others with him for the journey. Where one might expect opposition, Josh finds partners for the journey.

This is a book filled with hope — hope that the love we find in Christ can be exported to those our culture tells us to ignore, dislike, and expel. In this book, divisions become family, and people of other cultures and color become friends. The Old Testament story does not have to end with Abraham expelling Ishmael for Isaac's sake. Josh has chosen a New Testament ending to an old story: where Isaac doesn't fear Ishmael, where he seeks out Ishmael, where he calls Ishmael his brother.

You would do well to read *Engaging Nineveh*, and you would be much better to emulate what you have read.

Nik Ripken
International Mission Board Missionary, Author

ENGAGING NINEVEH

A Conservative Church, a Baptist Preacher,
and a Newfound Heart for Muslims

Section 1

Chapter 1

Look Around

I drove north on Interstate 85, heading for home on a muggy, summer day in central North Carolina. Tears streamed down my face as I wrestled with God.

I rarely cry, although I am getting softer with each passing year. I have watched a dazzling bride dressed in white, walking down the aisle to become my wife, but only grinned with excitement. I witnessed the birth of my three beautiful children and felt joy beyond measure, but shed no tears. I have endured the tragic passing of those I love and felt gripped inside, but did not cry. Many may consider me calloused because these occasions did not move me to tears. On that northbound drive, however, I wept.

I left Southeastern Baptist Theological Seminary in Wake Forest, North Carolina, after a weeklong intensive class. Approaching the home stretch of my Master of Divinity track, I needed one more elective course. As I scanned the summer schedule a few months before, I saw a class on Christian persecution.

International Mission Board missionaries Nik and Ruth Ripken were the instructors. Their names caught my eye because I had recently read their first book, *The Insanity of God*. Their story opened my eyes to the state of the church. Ripken recounted their journeys as missionaries all over the world, interviewing persecuted Christians. I could not put the book down. Their life story and the accounts of persecuted Christians riveted my soul.

On the first day of class, I anticipated meeting the Ripkens. I had never seen Nik Ripken before, and I did not know what to expect. When I saw Nik, I saw a man who appeared physically worn. He had difficulty with his knees and experienced several other health issues because of his extensive travels. But God greatly used him that week. He sat in a chair and recounted amazing stories of courageous men and women whom he had interviewed in his journeys. He challenged us to see the world of missions differently.

His wife, Ruth, also blessed the class. She was warm and kind and glowed with God's love. She also spoke during the week, and they both opened our eyes to all God was doing in the dark places around the world.

Their accounts broke my heart, but another element of their teaching troubled my heart even more. Nik educated us about the Muslim regions of the world. He told how the New Testament church over the centuries had failed to take the gospel to Muslim regions. In his experience as a missionary, he found Muslims were open to the gospel if Christians would share it. Ripken reiterated that Christians have kept Jesus to themselves in the Islamic parts of the world. God's people had refused to go to those regions, leaving the Muslim world neglected for too long. His statements shook me.

The tears that coursed down my face during my drive home came from the challenge Ripken gave the class toward the end of the week. He illustrated it with the following statement: "Jonah was called to go to Nineveh, but Nineveh is now coming to us."

Ripken further explained the statement by saying that Muslims from all over the world are moving to the United States to start new lives. Although God has called us to go to them, God is also sending them to us. We have an obligation issued by Jesus in the Great Commission (Matthew 28:19-20) to engage them and share the gospel. Nik challenged me to look around in my community and see the Muslim field of harvest.

I wept because that week God used the Ripkens to open my eyes to the undeniable opportunity facing me. I felt ashamed that I hated Muslims. I cringed that I only witnessed to people who looked and lived as I did. I felt overwhelmed and ashamed that I was not seeing the mission field in my own community. I had been blind in many ways.

I pulled off the road and begged God for forgiveness. I was on a northbound highway, but I was on a spiritual highway that led me to see my world differently. I saw Nineveh in my neighborhood. I was on a journey to engage the Muslims in my American community with the gospel. Jesus saved me when I was nine years old, but on that northbound highway, He opened my eyes.

Some may think my testimony is overly dramatic, but that day began my current journey. That was the week God helped me to love my enemies. Because of a seminary class, that was the week I began loving Muslims for the first time. God's Spirit used a seminary class and faithful servants to open my eyes.

My travels in the weeks that followed reinforced God's message. The Southern Baptist Convention took place in Houston, Texas, that summer. As a typical SBC preacher's kid, I had grown up going to conventions. Many pastors planned their family vacations around the annual convention, and my dad was no exception.

This year, though, I went as a messenger because I served on staff. I found myself once again riding in the back seat, accompanying my parents to the convention, but this time as an adult sharing a rental car. Anywhere my parents wanted to go on our way back from the convention center, I went too.

My mother loves to shop at Walmart and Ross in every city she visits. I tell her they are virtually the same in every city, but to no avail. One evening, as we returned to the hotel from the convention center, my dad pulled into a Ross parking lot in Houston. I decided to wait in the car and text my wife, Jaclyn. My dad took the keys and, in a matter of minutes, the Houston heat got to me. I decided to go inside and get the keys so I could use the air conditioner. When I passed through the Ross entrance,

I did not see Texas. I saw the Middle East. Women in Middle Eastern attire peppered the entire store. I saw Middle Eastern men shopping and women browsing through the dress racks, all accompanied by scores of children.

I asked myself, "Isn't this Houston, Texas?" For the first time, I felt like a minority. I would have expected to see this in Cairo, Damascus, or Baghdad. I would not even have been shocked to witness this scene in New York City or Dearborn, Michigan. But in Houston?

As I spent that week in Texas, God opened my eyes to a modern-day Nineveh in Houston. I saw Muslims in department stores, restaurants, hotels, and gas stations. When I thought of Houston, I thought of Baptist cowboys, not Muslim women in hijabs. Just as Nik Ripken had said a few weeks before, the foreign mission field was now in our cities and communities.

Growing up in a mission-minded church, I had often heard that we are missionaries and that our neighborhoods were mission fields. When I heard that as a child in Sunday school, I always associated it with people who resembled me: white southern Americans. Now, those truths took on a new dimension.

When I googled the Muslim population in the United States, I learned my eyes had not deceived me in that Ross store. Houston had an extensive population of Muslims. In 2006, the Washington Post listed Houston as having the seventh largest Muslim population. More recently, the Muslim Academy listed Houston as having the second largest Muslim population in America. Calculating religion in a population is not an exact science, but Houston remains among the top ten places for Muslims to reside.

The reality of this remained as I returned home and saw Muslims working in various places in my community. We pay closer attention when we are passionate about something. My wife says I am obsessed with Chevy Silverado trucks. I constantly look at the latest models on my smartphone. My son, Gracen, shares this passion, so we point out each

Silverado we see driving down the road. I can also spot a Clemson Tiger paw on a car or sweatshirt from yards away because I am passionate about Clemson football. As God continues to cultivate my passion for Muslims in America, I notice them everywhere.

Our church leadership held a retreat in Lancaster, Pennsylvania, a few months after my trip to Houston. Some of our deacons and I patronized a local diner for supper. Our server looked Middle Eastern, so I asked her courteously where she was from. She told me she was from Lebanon and had lived in Lancaster for five years. Through further dialogue, I learned her parents owned the restaurant. We met them and found them to be hospitable and warm. We had a great connection and a pleasant experience. I left the diner chuckling. I commented to my wife, "When I think of Lancaster, PA, I think of Dutch Amish and whoopie pies but not Lebanese restaurant owners." She agreed.

Maybe I live in a bubble — and maybe this is not shocking to others — but God showed me something I had never seen before. As I researched Muslim populations in America, I wondered if, like me, others in the Christian community went through their church motions and wore blinders. In front of my eyes, an opportunity to touch unreached people groups evolved. I did not have to get on a plane to find them. I simply had to go to a diner and eat a club sandwich to find someone unengaged with the gospel. Or I could take my wife to Ross or Walmart. Once I looked around, I saw Nineveh ... the nations. I saw the uttermost parts of the earth in the innermost communities of my life. I saw Samaria and the uttermost parts of the earth in my Jerusalem.

Why should my story matter? One mistake we can make is thinking that sins are just committed. If we don't steal, lie, lust, and covet, we are safe. In some Christian circles, if we avoid cursing, drinking, smoking, and voting for the wrong political party, we please God. We think sin is something we do, but sin is also failing to do what God commands. And not noticing lost people around us is a treasonous sin.

The first challenge of this book is to call the reader to look around

… to wake up and notice. The lost nations Jesus refers to in the Great Commission are living, shopping, working, retiring, and dying right in our backyards, and we need to notice them.

We have the life-giving antidote for eternal separation from God. If we believe this, we are responsible for sharing God's love with the nations God has placed at our doorstep. The first step is to see the different races and cultures in our cities, communities, and neighborhoods.

Chapter 2

Look at Recent Decades

Everyone I know remembers where they were on September 11, 2001. That day becomes more of a faded memory in my mind but remains forever etched there, nevertheless. I was a typical Bible college student on that dreadful day. I got up early, feeling groggy because I had been up late studying the night before. I was the insane human being who signed up for the morning Old Testament Survey class. I had an exam that morning, so I sat in the classroom, scrambling to do one final review of my study notes.

One of my classmates entered the room and told me the World Trade Center tower had been hit by an airplane. I did not think much of it, assuming it was an accidental plane crash. The professor came in and administered the exam as if the world had not stopped turning. As I left the classroom and proceeded into the hallway, one of my best college friends, Chris Phelps, stopped me. Chris and I had become great friends because our last names had constantly placed us near each other. Sometimes people called me Phelps and called him Phillips. This was hilarious because, politically, we were on the opposite sides of the spectrum. We argued all the time about political issues but remain great friends.

Chris looked like Woody Harrelson's double. He always sported a polo golf shirt and an old ragged yellow Georgia Tech hat. I rarely saw him without it and accused him of sleeping in it. I loved Phelps because he always spoke his mind, and I always had fun around him.

I distinctly remember him breaking the updated news. "Phillips, did you hear?"

"I heard about that plane thing," I answered.

"Yes, but a second plane hit the other tower, and another plane hit the Pentagon. The news said that yet another plane was possibly heading for the White House, and the White House is being evacuated," Chris said.

"Did you say the White House?"

"Yes, this is crazy. They say it is a terrorist attack."

My other friend, Rocky, walked up and said, "Yeah, and if they attack the Grand Ole Opry, it's ooonnn!"

You have to know my middle Tennessee country friend, Rocky, to understand that statement. He was as country as sweet tea and cornbread, and the scary part is, he was serious. None of us fully grasped the gravity of the unfolding events.

I asked again, "Did you say the White House?"

"Yeah, why?" Chris asked.

"My dad is at the White House today!"

On the previous night, my dad had called to rub it in that he was going to the White House. He received an invitation as a pastor and Christian educator to meet with some members of the White House staff, along with other pastors. He also said he might meet Vice President Dick Cheney. I told him I was jealous, and I wished him well.

As I stood in the hallway that morning talking to my friends, I remembered the previous night's conversation and felt a drop in the pit of my stomach. I went outside and called Dad on his cell phone. The lines were down. I called my mother to see if she had heard from him. My college friends and I watched the news with apocalyptic horror as the towers collapsed and the New York skyline smoked with fire and ash. I remember thinking this is how the end of the world will feel. It took a couple of hours to contact someone from home. Dad was fine, and I was relieved.

Dad later explained how the events unfolded that day. He entered the White House and waited for the meeting to begin. Suddenly, Secret Service agents rushed into the room and evacuated all the meeting attendees. They ran into the street and saw smoke rising in the distance from the Pentagon flames. My dad and the other pastors prayed with the White House office staff while sitting on the street curb.

One year later, my father received an invitation to return to the White House on September 10, 2002. He thought he was attending the same meeting with the Secretary of Education, but as they sat and waited, President George W. Bush entered the room and spent a few moments with them. He expressed his appreciation to them for praying with his office staff during the crisis one year earlier. He took the time to thank them personally. They prayed and fellowshipped, and Dad now has a special memory that began with the tragedy we know as 9/11.

After 9/11, I felt confused, afraid, grieved, and outraged. I was ready for war, and I relished the thought of our US military "lighting up their world like the Fourth of July," as Toby Keith put it. I remember the songs promoting revenge and patriotism, the Presidential addresses, and the piles of rubble in New York City. I remember the brave men and women of the NYPD and the FDNY. I remember the roller-coaster emotions felt by all. For the first time in my life, I identified a real enemy: Muslims. I had no regard for the well-being of those in Iran, Iraq, Afghanistan, Pakistan, Syria, and Palestine. I look back on those days as times I wanted justice for those innocent Americans who died.

That feeling of brokenness still burns within me when I think of those lost on that day. But I see those events differently now. Some feelings I still hold. I still love my country, the men and women in our military, and our first responders. I still want justice in this world. I want the innocent protected and the guilty punished.

The only difference between my feelings then and now is the feelings I hold toward my enemies. I now have the same love for Muslims as I do anyone else. My heart breaks for my enemies. The more I study the Bible and engage my Muslim neighbors, the clearer my love for them becomes. What changed? My heart.

I share this before I reveal another reality: Muslims are moving to America in vast numbers. Instead of fearing them, I hope all of us can view this immigration of the post-9/11 world as an opportunity to fulfill the Great Commission, not as a time to hide in fear.

Pew Research Center projects that by 2050 the Muslim population will equal the Christian population and that by 2070, Muslims will outnumber Christians on a global scale. Pew Research also projects that by 2030, the Muslim population will more than double in the United States. They credit this increase in the US to two factors: immigration and Muslim birthrates.[1]

Before I researched the statistics of the Muslim population in America, I thought most Muslims in America lived in New York City, Detroit, and Los Angeles. And while those locations witness significant Muslim populations, the Muslim population is larger in places I did not expect. New York possesses the largest Muslim population in the United States but is followed by Maryland and Georgia.[2] Two of the top three states with the highest Muslim population are found below the Mason Dixon line.

According to an article by Islam Academy, of the top five cities with the highest Muslim populations in America, three of them are in the Bible Belt. The article has Houston, Texas, ranking second; Atlanta, Georgia, ranking third; and Washington, D.C., ranking fourth behind New York City, which is listed as number one.[3] All of these cities are becoming more diverse.

Texas hosts 250,000 Muslims. This figure makes up 6 percent of the state population. Muslims in Dallas, Houston, and Fort Worth have built several mosques and schools *(madrasas)*. Muslim women who work in police stations wear hijabs. The term "Muslim Texan" is now commonly used.[4]

The Muslim population is also growing rapidly in Georgia, especially in Atlanta. Thirty places of worship exist in Georgia, and the state has three well-known Quran schools.[5]

Northern Virginia has witnessed a rapid influx of Muslims since it is a suburb of Washington, D.C. Since 2000, the Muslim population has increased 12 percent in Alexandria, Virginia; 14 percent in Arlington, Virginia; 14 percent in Fairfax, Virginia; and 49 percent in Prince William. All these increases have occurred since 2000, and similar increases have occurred in the D.C. suburbs of Maryland.[6]

The city of Louisville boasts a Muslim population of five to ten thousand. Louisville hosts numerous Islamic organizations that represent many different Islamic ethnicities. The city also has many Muslim-owned businesses and restaurants.[7]

In the heart of the southern United States lies Nashville, Tennessee, known for country music, the Grand Ole Opry, and Andrew Jackson's Hermitage Plantation. Nashville is increasingly becoming more diverse each year. In 2013, an article written by New York Times reporter Kim Severson singled out Nashville as one of the up-and-coming diverse cities.[8] In the last two decades, Nashville has received 50,000 immigrant residents.[9] Among the increasing influx of immigrants are Kurdish Muslims. Many in the American Kurdish community know Nashville as little Kurdistan.[10]

I singled out Nashville because Nashville is an important city to many Christians. Nashville is not only the "buckle" of the Bible Belt, but it is also a city known for Christian publishers such as Lifeway and Broadman and Holman Publishers. In the heart of Christian literature distribution, we can see Kurds and many other ethnicities moving into the same communities.

Muslim increases occur not only in urban centers like Nashville and Houston but also in small-town America. One of the most diverse communities in the South is in Clarkston, Georgia. This small town outside of Atlanta, Georgia, has seen immigrants from many different countries move to their town. In an article written in 2013 by Hunter

Wallace of occidentaldissent.com, the mayor of Clarkston boasts of having fifty countries represented in their local high school. He also reported that the local Muslim mosques host eight hundred visitors for prayer each week.

In December 2017, an article in USA Today said that 11,500 businesses located on the West Coast have relocated their headquarters and factories to southern states. All these relocations took place since 2011.[11] This means a trending population shift to the southern parts of the United States is occurring. With this shift, we will see other ethnicities move to the southern states to find work in various corporations. This population shift will affect the academic triangle in North Carolina and the new business boom in Greenville and Spartanburg, South Carolina, and will, in turn, affect Muslim populations.

"Dixie" as we know it is changing. Many may see these shifts as threats to our way of life, but I see these population shifts as Great Commission opportunities. I see them now through spiritual eyes rather than the fleshly lenses I once looked through.

Other numbers illustrate a new way of looking at the changing times. Sadly, missionaries rarely touched the Middle Eastern regions of the world in the first twelve and a half centuries following the inception of Islam. Missionaries have journeyed to the Islamic Middle Eastern countries, but they have reported no major revival movements.

However, in the last two decades, God has moved among Islamic parts of the world. Mission experts now point to an influx of spiritual activity in Islamic regions. David Garrison, in his book, *A Wind in the House of Islam*, defines a spiritual movement as one thousand conversions and one hundred churches established.[12] In his research, he claims there have been sixty-nine spiritual movements in the world in the past two decades.[13] This is a drastic increase from previous centuries.

Research from Garrison and others reveals a major spiritual shift. The Holy Spirit is gradually moving among the Muslim populations of the world. When I read about this trend, I saw something I had never considered. The tragedy of 9/11 happened twenty-one years ago. When I view the events of 9/11 and the spiritual trends of the past two decades, I see a demonic move by Satan to stop the trends of God's revival in Muslim regions and drive a wedge between the Christian West and the Islamic East.

Satan knew this act of war would fuel division and hate between American Christians and Muslims. Islam is not just a Middle Eastern religion. More Muslims reside in Southeast Asia than in any other part of the world. Satan saw the pendulum shift and the wind of the Spirit blowing to Islamic peoples, and he acted swiftly to stifle the evangelism connection between the two groups.

I believe Satan uses extreme acts of terror for two purposes: to kill the innocent and to divide one culture from another. He desires to immobilize Christians in America, Europe, Asia, and Africa with fear and hate. He must separate Christians and Muslims to conquer Muslim followers. Terrorism is a part of his grand strategy to prevent 1.6 billion Muslims in the world from hearing about Jesus. If we view Muslims as dangerous and unreachable, then we are less likely to engage them with the gospel.

Spiritual awareness regarding this battle triggers key questions for believers. Among them are the following: Has Satan's strategy worked in your life? Are you scared of Muslims? Do you hate Muslims? Do you care about their eternal destiny? Has 9/11 pushed you further away from a Muslim or drawn you closer?

The last two decades show God moving among Muslims and Muslims moving closer to us. We can see this as an obstacle or an opportunity. Everything changed after 9/11, but what Satan meant for evil God can use for good.

Initially, when I looked into my heart and saw what was happening, I did not like what I saw, and it led me to repent. All of us must consider if fear and hate reside in our hearts for people who are not like us. Do we despise people of other races, religions, or cultures? Are we tempted to isolate ourselves and withdraw from society?

We also need to see the changing demographics in our nation. Communities are different. My community is different than your community. Suburbs can be diverse or composed of one race. When we research our cities, counties, and state demographics, we will probably be amazed at how the population has shifted. Some communities change slower than others, but state demographics usually change faster.

We also need to look at what God is doing around the world to bring people from non-Christian cultures to Himself, especially the conversion numbers in Muslim countries. When we see where the Spirit of God is moving the most, we gain hope for the future. God is on the move.

Chapter 3

Look at the Giants

My daughter, Nora, is a portrait of beauty, with long, beautiful dark blond hair and stunning ocean blue eyes. As her father, I am biased but agree with others who praise her beauty. She is a smart young girl, who, like a sponge, remembers whatever she hears. She learns from her Sunday school teachers and childcare workers at our church. Now and then, Nora, as well as my other two children, teach me more than I can learn in a seminary classroom. They teach me the most by reminding me of foundational truths I sometimes forget.

One day, as we drove home from school, she made a simple but profound statement — and one of the most truthful ones I have ever heard. "Daddy, did you know God is bigger than Goliath?"

I said, "Yes, He is, honey!" How often we forget God is bigger than any giant we face.

I grew up in church, and I have been in full-time church ministry for many years. I believe one of the biggest giants Christians face is the fear of sharing their faith. Barna's research reveals that only 52 percent of born-again Christians share their faith within a year.[14] This indicates the church is dropping the ball in witnessing. Along with fear, some do not witness because they feel they lack biblical knowledge. Others simply forget the gospel's value in their lives. Overcoming fear and sharing our faith can be like facing Goliath.

One of the toughest phases of evangelism is getting started and taking the first step to talk with someone. Starting a conversation or stepping over the threshold into another person's space is difficult for many people. I struggle with that also. Many find it difficult enough to share the gospel with a person who is culturally and ethnically similar to them, but to share the gospel with a Muslim can increase our anxiety.

We avoid crossing cultural barriers and work within our comfortable circles. I once listened to Matt Chandler, pastor of The Village Church in Fort Worth, Texas, preach from Ephesians 2 on the topic of ethnic diversity. He made a statement that stuck with me. He said, "We naturally drift toward the mirror," meaning that our natural inclination entails gravitating toward those who look like us. But the gospel is about all nations receiving the good news.

The Great Commission at its core involves cross-cultural engagement, which comes from going to all the nations (Matthew 28:19). In Acts 1:8, Jesus instructs the early church to witness in Jerusalem, Judea, Samaria, and the uttermost parts of the earth. All cultures and races have been privileged to hear the message, but that commission is marked by cultural awkwardness. To the Jewish hearer in Bible times, the thought of Jews going to Samaritans and Gentiles was foreign to their traditions as well as their fleshly natures.

I believe the same awkward feelings exist today with our Muslim neighbors, creating a wall. The wall is sometimes social awkwardness, sometimes fear, and sometimes both. Fear grips us in the West as the Muslim population increases. By 2017, the Muslim population in America had soared to 3.45 million. Pew Research predicts it will reach 8.1 million by 2050.[15] Many Christians in America fear an Islamic takeover in the West — that America will follow Europe, and the wars over Sharia law will infiltrate our American landscape. One in three Americans worries about Sharia law implementation in America.[16]

These fears cause many Americans to react violently. In 2001, after 9/11, reports revealed ninety-three assaults against Muslims. Violent incidents have remained steady throughout the past two decades. During 2015 and 2016, Muslim hate crimes spiked to 19 percent. In 2016 alone,

307 incidents of harassment occurred toward Muslims in America.[17]

Three Muslim students in Chapel Hill, North Carolina, were fatally shot in 2015. Following that tragedy, other acts were reported across the country, prompting concerns that the anti-Muslim sentiments were increasing.[18] Muslim advocates blame the Islamophobia attitudes of Americans on news coverage that fails to separate armed terror groups from Muslims. In their opinion, the media lumps all terror groups and Muslims in the same category.[19] Half of the Muslims polled say it has become harder to be a Muslim in the US in recent years. A 2017 poll revealed that 48 percent of Muslims say they have experienced at least one incident of discrimination in twelve months.[20]

In contrast, most Americans do not feel Muslims receive unfair treatment. A Rasmussen poll recorded that since 2011, 63 percent of Americans do not feel Muslims are being treated unfairly.[21] Americans also feel Muslims are a welcomed people group in America as it relates to religious freedom. Fifty-seven percent of Americans believe the US is a welcoming place for Muslims.[22] The data indicates that the two sides are at polar extremes over this issue.

At the same time, evangelicals take a step back because of reservations about the Islamic religion. Two-thirds of American pastors view Islam as a dangerous religion. Lifeway research of one thousand Protestant pastors found that 45 percent strongly agree that Islam is dangerous, and 21 percent agreed somewhat.[23] Nabeel Qureshi, a former Pakistani Muslim and a convert to Christianity, wrote a book entitled *Understanding Jihad* just before his death in 2017. He explained that until the nineteenth century, Islam was historically violent and that Muslims were perfectly comfortable calling Islam a religion of violence.[24]

Muslims claim violence will cease and peace will reign in Islam if there is a reformation in Islam, somewhat like the Protestant Reformation in Europe. However, Qureshi warned that, if Islam reforms, it will grow more violent because violence remains in the origins of Islamic doctrine.[25] If that is the case, Al Qaida, ISIS, and Boko Haram are the true reformers of Islam today.

I agree that Islam is a dangerous religion when practiced literally, but not all Muslims are dangerous. Christians must rise above these battle lines in our society. The question Christians must ask doesn't regard the dangers of Islam. We should be concerned about Muslims. Most Muslims do not want to hurt anyone. A Gallup poll conducted after 9/11 revealed that 91 percent of Muslims interviewed believed the attacks were morally unjustified. In fact, 358 Muslim employees died in the World Trade Center that day.[26]

In his book, *Breaking the Islam Code*, J.D. Greear wrote, "I found my Muslim neighbors and friends to be some of the kindest people on earth. ... Most desire, but will never have a Christian friend."[27]

In my work with Muslims in America, I found that Muslims vehemently oppose terrorism and even claim terrorists do not practice true Islam. My work may represent only a small sample and may be highly debated by many, but that has been my experience. Some Muslims seek violence, but they are a small minority. The majority in America are here to live the American dream, not destroy it. They are in America for employment, an education for their children, and quality medical care.

I once had some dear friends to whom I taught English. They were Syrian refugees and came to America through the lottery process. They had five children and were sweet people. I asked them why they left Syria. They stared at me as though I had asked the most ridiculous question of all time. The toils of war had destroyed their home. Their lives were under constant threat of destruction. They simply answered, "We are safe here, and we now have a future." This was their story, and it is the story of thousands of Muslims living in Europe and the United States.

A good Christian friend of mine once stated something in a group that caused me to shudder. We were discussing the Muslim ministry I was involved in, and he looked at me jovially and said, "It would suit me fine if we just dropped a bomb on every Muslim country and made it a parking lot because they are evil."

Everyone listening laughed, but not me. I said, "If evil is the criteria, then God could start right here in our town." Others have probably heard statements such as, "We should just kill them all and let God sort them out," or "I hope to send them to their ten virgins." Jesus died for everyone, Muslims included, and, if we are like Jesus, then statements like that conflict with Jesus' death on the cross.

I believe we should protect our citizens and bring justice for evil actions. But we cannot let politics blind us to God's kingdom purpose. We must seek first the kingdom of God. We must fight this giant with the sling of the gospel and the five smooth stones of love, peace, patience, kindness, and gentleness. We have a message for them to hear, but we must overcome the giant of fear and talk to them.

I know terrorists seek to hurt innocent people. I know ISIS and many other hate-filled people seek to kill thousands in the name of Allah. Terrorists are the weapons of the giant we face in today's world. This giant of fear disables Christians and keeps them away from Muslims.

Christopher Wright, in his book *The Mission of God*, says this is not a new problem. In both the Old and New Testaments, God's people struggled to share their faith with foreign people, even though the Bible commands us to reach across cultural barriers with the gospel.[28] He writes, "For two thousand years, Christian missions, ever since the New Testament church, has wrestled with the problems of multiple cultural contexts."[29] This is not a new villain, just one wearing a different mask. When David was about to face a giant, he questioned if there were not a cause. I ask the same question about this giant causing fear among God's people. In the words of my daughter, "God is bigger than Goliath!"

Section 2

Chapter 4

Look in Scripture

Inspired by Nik and Ruth Ripken, I saw Muslims on American soil. I looked at the recent decades and saw the events of the world and the movements of God within Muslim communities. I saw terrorism as a weapon of Satan to subvert the Great Commission. I looked at the giants of fear and prejudice that obstruct our sharing Christ with Muslims. My journey led me to the Bible, where the answers to all questions that matter are found.

The great London preacher, Charles Spurgeon, once challenged all preachers to have a Bible in one hand and a newspaper in the other. He charged preachers to be current on world affairs and to address world events with a biblical worldview. In sad contrast, I once heard a preacher tell me he only read the Bible. He did not read any other books and paid little attention to the news. He said, "The Bible is all I need."

I believe the Bible is the inerrant Word of God. I also believe it is the greatest book ever written. I also believe Spurgeon was right. We must know what is going on around us and be God's mouthpiece in a turbulent world. The old saying "Christians can be so heavenly minded that they are no earthly good" applies. We must view the world through the biblical lenses of the Bible. We must see world events that unfold and then read the Bible to know how to be light in a world of darkness.

Updating Spurgeon's statements, I would say all Christians should walk through life with their cellphones in one hand and their Bibles in the other. Of course, the situation has flipped somewhat in my mind. We have our smartphones in one hand, but I wonder if we have the Bible in the other hand.

My experience as a pastor, coupled with conversations I have had with more experienced pastors, tells me this may be a universal problem. A lack of biblical knowledge appears to exist among Christians. I especially see a lack of biblical application. The Bible works as the greatest guide in any situation. The Bible is timeless and is a lamp to our feet and a light to our path — but only when applied.

My journey to engage and evangelize Muslims had a statistical layer as I looked at the numbers of Muslims in America, but my quest also had a scriptural layer. I wanted to know what the Bible declared about loving Muslims. As I saw the Muslim issues in America, and the world crisis regarding terrorism, I turned to the Bible as my guide to understanding this polarizing issue. I hoped to find God's will for the Muslims and the people of the Middle East. I also wanted to know how to share the gospel with them.

I grew up in a pro-Israel family and church. My home church sanctuary posts the Israeli flag next to the American flag. I was taught that Israel is the favored and chosen people of God and that we must help Israel at all costs. God promised Abraham He would bless those who blessed Abraham and curse those who cursed him. Additionally, all the families of the earth would be blessed through him (Genesis 12:3). I believed a friend of Israel received a blessing from God, while an enemy of Israel received a curse from God.

The conflict between Muslims and Jews has global ramifications for every nation. My pro-Israel upbringing caused me to develop an either-or mentality. I once felt that to associate with a Muslim was to betray the Jews because the Middle Eastern world's rhetoric was so anti-Israel. To some, these views might seem silly. I had to come to grips with these issues. God liberated me from these types of strongholds. I now see things differently.

I still love Israel because God birthed my Savior from Zion, because

Jesus loves Israel, and because the Apostle Paul loved them. I want all Jews to come to Christ, just as Paul did (Romans 9). I believe God has a plan for the children of Isaac (Jews), but I also believe He has a plan for the children of Ishmael (Muslims). As I surveyed the Bible and asked for God's guidance, I found the best starting place was the story of Hagar and Ishmael. God is not finished with the children of Ishmael. They, too, have a future.

I connect Muslims to Ishmael because of historical traditions. The term Muslim never appears in the Bible. Muhammad and the founding of Islam do not appear on the timeline of history until AD 570-632.[30] The precise date given in history is AD 610, but great debate exists among Muslims about when Islam began.[31] Muhammad's birth follows the conclusion of the New Testament by five hundred years.

Islam began in Mecca, the birthplace of Muhammad and the place Muslims believe Ishmael founded.[32] Historians credit Ishmael as the father of the Arab race.[33] The Quran is recited and read in the Arabic language all over the world. Muslims, Hebrews, and Christians consider Muslims as descendants of Ishmael.[34] For these reasons, I connect Muslims and Ishmael.

In Genesis 16, the inception of the great conflict between the two sons of Abraham began. Hagar and Ishmael entered the picture of God's narrative in chapters 16 and 21. By agreement with his wife Sarah, Abraham impregnated Hagar, Sarah's handmaid, to produce an heir. Their act evidenced a lack of faith in God's promise to provide them with a child when circumstances appeared hopeless. This lapse in faith set into motion the conflict of the ages between the descendants of these two sons of Abraham.

Ishmael's birth preceded the arrival of Isaac, God's chosen seed. Even before the birth of Isaac, Sarah scolded Hagar harshly and caused her to run away in tears. This incident marks the first conflict between Hagar and Sarah. Hagar escaped to a desolate well, sat, and wept. During this episode, the Angel of the Lord appeared to Hagar and instructed her to return to Sarah.

The angel then made Hagar a promise: "Behold, you are with child, and you shall bear a son. You shall call his name Ishmael because the Lord has heard your affliction" (Genesis 16:11). God continued detailing Ishmael's future heritage by pronouncing his name and describing his characteristics. He would have a wild nature (the Hebrew word commonly translated as "wild" literally means wild donkey). He would also show independence and hostility toward others. This aggressive attitude would invite retaliation from his neighbors. Finally, he would act violently.[35]

Hagar and Ishmael are two clear man-made outcasts in the Bible. Sarah cast Hagar out of her presence, and a major schism formed within this family. Even though Hagar faced rejection by Sarah, God spoke to her in a time of sadness. God promised to make something great of an awkward situation. Ishmael would become a handful, but God would bless him regardless.

Despite Sarah's rejection of Hagar and Ishmael, God blessed Hagar and heard her cry out in her affliction. The word "affliction" refers to the Hebrew concept of misery.[36] Hagar named the place where God met her *Beer-lahai-roi*, which means "the well belonging to the Living One who has seen me."[37] These names are symbolic. The name Ishmael means, "God hears."[38] Hagar declares the truth of the ages. In our desperation, God, the Living One, hears. In our brokenness, God, the Living One, sees.

The story continues in Genesis 21. The Angel of God reassured Hagar of God's promise. Sarah birthed Isaac, the child God had promised to Abraham. After Isaac's birth, the rivalry between Sarah and Hagar intensified. Abraham submitted to Sarah's demand to banish Hagar and Ishmael from their camp. Abraham agonized over the decision, but God reassured him that he would make a nation from Ishmael because Ishmael was also his seed.

Hagar journeyed into the wilderness of Beer-sheeba. The supply of water for her and Ishmael depleted, and their future appeared bleak. In desperation, Hagar cried out to the Lord for help, and, again, God heard her cry and provided a well.

In Genesis 16 and 21, the Angel of God met Hagar and provided life-giving water in the desert. These incidents give an interesting picture of salvation. Water is the symbolic picture of salvation in Hagar's desperate need. Arab Muslims today view this well of water as a well of monumental significance. According to Arab tradition, the well of Zamzam near the land of Ka'ba, which is fed by an underground spring, constitutes the oasis given by God to Hagar.

I have learned to value the beautiful pictures in the Old Testament of salvation, sacrifice, atonement, and redemption. The Old Testament is riddled with pictures of Christ and salvation. Christological types are interwoven in this narrative also.

This well symbolized things to come for the children of Ishmael. In Genesis 22, God arranged a ram with his head caught in a thicket as a picture of salvation for Abraham and Isaac. The ram was the sacrifice provided by the Angel of the Lord to take the place of Isaac, Abraham's beloved son. Just as God provided a sacrifice in Genesis 22, God provided water in Genesis 21. The symbol of hope for Hagar and Ishmael was the oasis of water that saved them from death. The symbols are different, but each was evidence that God wanted to save both sons of Abraham.

Old Testament scholar Kenneth Mathews points out the picture of Christ that also exists with the Angel of the Lord in the text. The Angel of the Lord in Genesis 22 with Abraham and Isaac and the Angel of God with Hagar and Ishmael in Genesis 21 are both Christ types. We see Jesus at work with both sons of Abraham. Isaac was the heir with a blessed promise, but Ishmael was the son of Abraham with a separate promise.

These stories tie into the relationship between Christians and Muslims. Both of Abraham's sons are involved with the gospel. The descendants of Isaac would bring Jesus to deliver the gospel, and the descendants of Ishmael would be recipients of the gospel.

The importance of the gospel in the life of the outcast spoke to me.

Ishmael and his mother were outcasts in the house of Abraham. Jesus came to seek the outcast. One of the beautiful aspects of the gospel is the merciful invitation God extends to the Gentile and the most downtrodden. He came to set people free and hear their cries.

Paul emphasizes this in his letter to the Ephesians when he talks about how far the Ephesians were from God. That also applies to us. "Therefore remember that you, once Gentiles in the flesh — who are called Uncircumcision by what is called the Circumcision made in the flesh by hands — that at that time you were without Christ, being aliens from the commonwealth of Israel and strangers from the covenants of promise, having no hope and without God in the world. But now in Christ Jesus you who once were far off have been brought near by the blood of Christ" (Ephesians 2:11-13).

We are in the same category. We were outcasts from God until Jesus came to draw us close. Like Hagar and Ishmael, we are outcasts, but we can be adopted into God's family. The gospel promise gives us hope.

In the Sermon on the Mount, Jesus said, "Blessed are those who mourn, for they shall be comforted" (Matthew 5:4). Facing Mecca, the Muslim prays five times a day to Allah. Unfortunately, they pray to the wrong god. Jesus wants to hear their cry. The gospel is for them, and they need to hear the message. Jesus fulfills the promise with the gospel. Hagar and Ismael wanted water in a time of dry desperation. The Angel of the Lord (Jesus) heard their cry. He also hears the cries of their descendants today, but only the gospel will quench their thirst. We carry the water.

Christ calls Christians to share their faith with Muslims. Followers of Jesus have good news for the descendants of Ishmael. We have water that will save them in their spiritual desert. Although most Muslims are from other regions of the world, Islam originated from the children of Ishmael. Muslims have historically assumed that Muhammad descended from Ishmael.[39] When I see Muslims, I see the spiritual lineage and the connection. I especially see the connection when I engage with a Middle Eastern Muslim.

The last time Isaac and Ishmael stood together was at the graveside of Abraham, two sons with distinctly different futures. They shared the same father but different mothers and promises. Yet, both promises lead to the foot of the cross. God wants a family reunion. I believe that one day, at the feet of Jesus, the children of Isaac and Ishmael who have found salvation and cleansing through Jesus will worship together for all eternity.

John the Apostle records the great reunion of the nations (Revelation 7:9). Every tribe and tongue will worship God.[40] Arabs, Iranians, Palestinians, Iraqis, and Syrians will stand with the Jews at the feet of Jesus. They will all share a common denominator: faith in Christ. Abraham's two sons stood at his tomb in Genesis 25, but in heaven, their descendants will stand at the throne of a living Son. The reunion is coming, and I am excited about it.

Could it be that Jews and Middle Eastern Muslims will come back together as a family through the mediating work of Christians? Christ will bring the children of Isaac and Ishmael together, but He will use us to do it through the Great Commission mandate. God keeps His promises to both Isaac and Ishmael through the redemption of Jesus Christ. God is up to something extraordinary.

This story is a great starting place to have a gospel conversation with a Muslim. Tell them the story of Ishmael and Hagar's promise. This story works as a great launching pad to help Muslims identify with Christ. Hagar and Ishmael's promise is a great bridge story for a Christian woman befriending a Muslim woman. Make the connection. In my journey, this story has worked to open ears and hearts to Jesus. It is a story of beginnings. Look to the promise.

Chapter 5

Look at the Path to Water

At nineteen, I dreamed of taking a trip to Israel. My church scheduled a trip, and I longed to go. I remember praying for God to make it possible. I was a young man working construction and trying to pay my way through community college. I did not know how I would afford the trip.

God opened amazing doors, and I was able to go for little cost. The trip opened my eyes and affected the way I read the Bible. I saw the places I had learned about as a child: Galilee, Bethlehem, Jerusalem. I floated on the Dead Sea and was immersed in the Jordan River when baptized. My eyes beheld Gethsemane, Calvary, and the Garden Tomb. When a person sees these places, they never read the Bible in the same way because the images match the words of Scripture.

One place etched in my memory is Jacob's Well. This was the historical well situated where Jacob lived for twenty years. It is also the burial place of Joseph. The well is roughly four feet wide. In AD 670, a visitor wrote that the well was 240 feet deep. In 1697, a visitor said the well was 105 feet deep. In 1861, it was 75 feet deep. The depth has decreased because of the pebbles pilgrims have thrown into it over the centuries. Although the well is not as deep as it once was, it still has pure water inside.[41]

I descended the staircase to see the well and saw a tiny metal cup on the edge of it. I asked if I could have a drink from the well. The overseer of the well permitted me. I drew up a small bucket of water from the well, dipped the cup into the bucket, and took a drink. The water was pure and cold. Looking back on that, I think I was out of my mind to drink from that cup. The water was refreshing, but thinking about the number of germs on that cup from the thousands of people who had done the same thing before me now causes me to shudder.

This well is significant for another reason. This is the well where Jesus sat and engaged a Samaritan woman (John 4). The story stands out and provides tremendous insight into Jesus' compassionate nature. The story also teaches us about the importance of engaging lost people in daily life. The overall theme is that Jesus wants to give living water to this woman so she will never thirst again.

As I searched the Bible for guidance involving Muslim engagement and evangelism, this story came to mind. I saw many components that would help me in Muslim ministry, but I also saw many wonderful aspects that paralleled other events of Scripture. Jesus' approach was interesting. He purposefully chose to go to Samaria. Jews did not customarily travel through Samaria on their way to Galilee from Jerusalem because Jews traditionally viewed Samaritans as unclean people.[42]

The rift between Jews and Samaritans extended back centuries. Israelites of Northern Israel started marrying Assyrian invaders after 721 BC and, over the centuries, produced the Samaritan race. They were ethnically half Jew and half Gentile.

Jews and Samaritans were ethnic and religious rivals in the days of Jesus. The feuds were so deeply felt that Jews considered Samaritans as unclean inbreeds who had no place in Jewish communities. They were ethnically different but also held different religious views. Although they shared some things, significant religious differences remained. Samaritans accepted Assyrians' religious practices and intermingled them with Judaism.[43]

Jesus intentionally passed through Samaria despite the cultural barriers. His actions reflect God's character. God spoke light into a dark place when He said let there be light (Genesis 1:2-3).[44] God goes to places that we consider off-limits. Jesus shares God's character. The prophet Isaiah declares that beautiful prophecy of Jesus: "The people who walked in darkness have seen a great light; those who dwelt in the land of the shadow of death, upon them a light has shined" (Isaiah 9:2). John also writes, "And the light shines in the darkness, and the darkness did not comprehend it" (John 1:5). And Paul says Jesus made Himself of no reputation and took the form of a servant (Philippians 2:7). Jesus goes to off-limits places.

This is also the character of the Holy Spirit. John 14, Acts 1:8, and Acts 2 all refer to the coming of the Holy Spirit to a broken world. The Holy Spirit also goes to off-limits places. All three persons of the triune God show the willingness to come to earth. This willingness shows Jesus would not be limited by human understanding and cultural traditions. Jesus broke tradition on many occasions. He intentionally went to a place no other son of Abraham would go. He went to an out-of-bounds place. This is our God.

We must follow Jesus' example. To engage Muslims, we must go where they hang out. We must go to the Muslim's well. That may be coffee shops, public libraries, or places where Muslims shop.

Jesus also spoke to an outcast. He sat by the well of Jacob and engaged a Samaritan woman. This woman was off limits to any Jewish man. Jewish culture forbade a Jewish man to speak to a Samaritan woman. Her ethnicity was an issue. Although not a prostitute, she lived a sexually promiscuous lifestyle, having had five husbands and living at the time with a man who was not her husband.[45] Jesus knew about her baggage, her ethnicity, and the social rules, but He still shared the good news.

Talking to Muslims may frighten us, but God calls us to talk to those across social divides. The way they dress and their cultural differences may seem daunting, but be fearless. Seek to learn their cultural norms and work within those rules. The overall goal is to engage so we can one day evangelize. One caution: Men cannot speak to women, in most cases, in Muslim culture. But Christian men can engage Muslim men, and Christian women can engage Muslim women. The only hope for some Muslim women in America and around the world is to hear the gospel through the intentional engagement of Christian women.

I have tried to apply the principles I discovered in this story. I identified every Middle-Eastern-owned business in my community. I try to purchase gas, coffee, lunch, and other necessities from Muslim-owned businesses. I then cultivate a relationship with the Muslim owners.

I once stopped for a cup of coffee at one of the local Seven-Eleven stores in my town. The cashier was a young woman of Middle Eastern ethnicity. She wore a hijab covering her head. I purchased my items and thanked her. She was allowed to speak to me since this was a business transaction, so I asked her where she was from.

"Pakistan," she said.

"Great! How long have you lived in America?"

"Two years."

"Well, welcome to America. My name is Josh! What is yours?"

"Heba."

"Well, it is great to meet you, Heba. Do you and your family work here together?"

"Yes, my husband's name is Abdullah."

"Great. I hope to meet him next time."

This was a local well conversation. I planned to return there to meet her husband and cultivate a friendship with them. I will work that lead until God shuts the door. I must go through Samaria just as Jesus went through Samaria.

We may hear some say, "All these Muslims are taking over our local businesses, and I'm boycotting them. They need to go back to where they came from." This may be the worldview of some, and they may criticize us for talking to them, but we must go through Samaria.

Jesus pierced through religious differences. He did not fear this woman, although her religious views contrasted with His truth. Samaritans shared some common beliefs with traditional Judaism, but they differed on many religious components.

The woman asked Jesus about places of worship. The Jews believed

Jerusalem was the holy mountain of worship, but the Samaritans thought Mt. Gerizim was. Jesus spoke into those differences but took the conversation back to the most important points: Jesus the Messiah and living water.

Muslims hold major differences from Christians, and many of the differences will surface in theological conversations. The big differences are the death, burial, and resurrection of Jesus; the Trinity; the deity of Jesus; and salvation by grace through faith in Christ. As Paul reminded Timothy, we must study God's Word (2 Timothy 2:15). Peter reminds us we must also be equipped to defend it (1 Peter 3:15). Know what you believe and why.

When having a theological conversation with a Muslim, answer the questions honestly and humbly. When we are stumped by a question, we can be honest and tell them we do not know the answer but will find out. Honesty and humility go a long way. Like Jesus, do not be afraid to engage and always seek to share the gospel in the conversation. We can share the gospel by simply telling our testimony of how we came to faith in Christ. I have found that even the simplest testimony speaks volumes about the powerful love of Jesus.

I once volunteered at a local Muslim ministries to teach English classes to Syrian refugees in our city. We typically spent the first hour learning vocabulary words and writing sentences with those words. We then took a coffee break and continued the second session. In the second session, we talked to each other in English. Conversations helped them learn faster. We talked about our families, children, backgrounds, favorite foods, and favorite ice cream. These are just general conversations that help us get closer as a group and help the refugees learn English at the same time.

One day, I predetermined to share the gospel with them during our conversation time. I had been teaching classes for several weeks and had developed a good relationship. I felt the Lord leading me to share my story with them. I asked God to give me wisdom and clarity. I began our time by asking each of them to tell me how they became Muslim. They each told me their religious stories and how they were born into Islam. I asked questions about Islam. Keep in mind, I already knew some of the answers, but I was trying to break the ice.

After they told their stories, I asked if I could share my story. They wanted to hear. I always considered my testimony boring, but I shared how I had grown up in church and how God saved me when I was nine years old. I then explained how I bowed my knees, repented of my sins, and put my faith in Christ for salvation. I gave details of my story, and they sat quietly and listened intently. One part of my story got their attention. I told them that since I had become a Christian, I was at peace with God. They were interested in internal peace and seemed to crave the peace I possessed.

We had great dialogue that day, and Jesus filled the room with His presence. None of them believed in Jesus, but God worked in them. This is what I mean by having a theological conversation. Jesus was willing to have one with the Samaritan woman. We must be willing to emulate Jesus and have these conversations.

Jesus spoke to a woman rejected by the children of Abraham and offered her living water. This encounter is an interesting parallel to Hagar at the oasis. Both women were rejected, both were desperate, and both heard Jesus address their needs. Hagar cried out for help and Jesus answered, giving her life-sustaining water in her time of need. The Samaritan woman asked Jesus to give her living water that Jesus claimed would quench her thirst so that she would never thirst again (John 4:13-15).

I believe Muslims seek the same living water. A great debate exists about Sharia law. Many fear it will take over in the West, and Muslims do strive to live under this law to please Allah.

As I sought to understand the practices of Islam, I read many books on their culture and religion. During my journey, I stumbled upon the testimony of Nabeel Qureshi. He was a Muslim from birth and came to faith in Christ as an adult. He wrote two books that taught me about Muslim evangelism and culture. Reading his book, *Answering Jihad*, I was astounded by what I read about Sharia law. The term Sharia means literally "path to water."[46] When I studied the stories of Hagar and the Samaritan woman, I was stunned. Muslims are looking for water, but they are seeking it in the wrong places.

The more I study Islam, the more heartbroken I become. They are thirsty, but if they could just find Jesus, they would never thirst again. We have the good news to share with the thirsty. In February 1989, Christ quenched my thirst when I accepted Him by faith. I want the Muslim who is seeking water to find it. Hagar found it. The Samaritan woman found it. It is time for the Sharia-practicing Muslims to find that living water Jesus offers.

Jesus said, "Blessed are those who hunger and thirst for righteousness, for they shall be filled" (Matthew 5:6). The call to drink water is prevalent in how we identify with Christ. There are numerous songs about how our fountains are found in Christ, as well as songs that invite us to come and drink the living waters. As I saw these parallels in Scripture, I began to see water and living water everywhere — from songs to Scriptures to stories. God wants all to drink the living water.

I heard a story once of many Syrian and Iraqi refugees fleeing war-torn cities. Their houses had been destroyed. In that region of the world, mission organizations, with the help of volunteers, erected water stations so these refugees could obtain clean drinking water. While the refugees waited to receive water, missionaries shared the gospel with them. Hundreds accepted Christ as Savior. As I heard this report, I could not help but think of Hagar and the Samaritan woman. I also could not help but think of Sharia law and the irony. They were in line to get a drink of clean water, but they received both drinking water and living water at the same time. God is interested in those who are thirsty.

Some of the last words spoken in the Bible by John in Revelation call all who are thirsty to drink. John wrote, "And the Spirit and the bride say, 'Come!' And let him who hears say, 'Come!' And let him who thirsts come. Whoever desires, let him take the water of life freely" (22:17). I love that the Spirit and the bride both say come and that all who are thirsty can drink the water freely. We will bring living water to the Muslim world through the guidance and power of the Holy Spirit. May we all give living water to the thirsty.

The Samaritan woman at the well is another story to tell when having religious conversations with Muslims, especially with Muslim women. Nothing is more moving than a woman of faith telling this story to a Muslim woman. A Muslim woman can relate to the feeling of being an outcast because of her male-dominated culture. The Holy Spirit moves when stories are told from Scripture that speak to the heart. Muslim women are thirsty and want to be filled. Jesus wants to fill them, but we, the church, are the messengers.

Chapter 6

Look to Nineveh

A man I will call Abraham met me at The Cheesecake Factory for an interview. Abraham grew up in Iraq and was reared as a Muslim. Now, he is a devout follower of Christ. I had met him at a conference and was intrigued by his grasp of American Muslims and the knowledge of evangelism he had shared. After hearing him speak, I knew I needed to learn more from him.

After hearing my brief description of Abraham's story, one of my friends, Dave England, asked if he could tag along. We arrived early the next day and waited in the lounge area of the restaurant for Abraham's arrival. Abraham quietly and cautiously slipped into the front entrance. We made eye contact, and he approached me, looking somewhat apprehensive. I extended my hand, smiled, and thanked him for meeting me. Then, I introduced Dave. Abraham seemed cold and nervous, and he urged us to move to a table. We found a booth and began to talk. He apologized for the brisk introduction but informed me that he gets nervous in public because of his ministry work. Many extremists have threatened him.

After receiving our drinks, Abraham made an astonishing statement: "ISIS is the greatest tool God is using today to bring about the Great Commission to the Muslim world." I was taken aback by the statement but told him to continue.

He said, "Muslims are running for their lives to get away from this evil madness, and now they are seeking freedom from the chains. They are primed and ready to hear the good news of Jesus Christ." Abraham took a sip of his water with lemon and continued. "Hundreds of Muslims are professing their faith in Jesus because they know Islam is a religion of violence and death. We have a golden opportunity, if only American Christians could just see it."

I asked, "Do you have Muslims here in America coming to faith in Christ?"

"Absolutely, but bringing them to Christ is the easy part."

"What is the difficult part?"

"Getting them discipled and loved by Christians. You have to understand Middle Eastern cultures. Muslims value fellowship, family, and community. In Islam, they feel safe in their families and communities, and these things matter. But when Muslims profess faith in Christ, they are banished from their Muslim communities. Christians in America refuse to associate with them because of fear. The loneliest person in America is a former Muslim seeking a new Christian family. They need the church's embrace."

The conversation became one-sided. Dave and I were like sponges absorbing all Abraham said. He told his story of coming to faith in Christ. Abraham served in the Iraqi army under Saddam Hussein's regime. He served in the 1980s during the Iraqi war with Iran. Abraham was afraid he would die and did not have peace about his eternal destiny. He decided to become an Islamic imam, feeling this would seal his destiny in Paradise. He studied fervently but did not feel that even being an imam sufficed. He decided to become a Muslim missionary to evangelize Christians.

To understand the beliefs of Christians, he had to learn about Jesus. He read the passage in the Quran that speaks of Jesus being unable to tell a lie. This revelation led Abraham to find a Bible so he could study the four Gospels. He said, "I felt if Jesus could tell no lies, then I needed to read His words."

The reading of the Scripture led Abraham to faith in Christ. He later moved to the United States and now serves as a pastor among American

Muslims. His ministry has grown into a network of house churches.

In the meeting, we discussed many more aspects of Muslim engagement and evangelism. All that God showed us through this courageous man astonished Dave and me. As we finished our meal, I asked Abraham one final question. "Besides Jesus, what is the greatest need of the Muslims in America?"

"A friend. If Christians would show love and hospitality to the Muslims in their communities, they would evangelize many of them."

Driving home that afternoon, I asked Dave what he thought of the lunch. He said, "I have never experienced anything like that in my life."

I said, "It is like Christianity at a whole new level. It is like Christianity in high definition."

Dave and I were two lifelong Baptist-raised boys who needed to get out of our Bible Belt bubble.

As I processed what Abraham had said, I could not help but think about the statements regarding ISIS. I cannot think of a more malevolent, reprehensible group of people in the history of humanity. In my view, ISIS and the Nazis rival as the grossest perpetrators of evil toward innocent humanity in history. How could I possibly see ISIS as a blessing? I still, without question, see ISIS as the head of Satan, and I think the world would be a better place if they were defeated once and for all.

I submitted my feelings to God and asked Him to guide me to view these matters with His eyes. God directed me to the book of Jonah. Jonah remains one of the greatest mission accounts in the Bible. Scholars revel in the mission emphasis found in Jonah's story.[47] The revival that occurred in the pagan city of Nineveh remains the greatest revival in history. Just imagine the social media currents that would flow if 120,000 people in a city like New York, Los Angeles, Paris, or London converted to Christianity in one day. Fox News, CNN, Facebook, and Twitter would be on overload, posting the comments and interviewing the transformed.

This revival was not the result of a great prophet. Jonah was a disobedient, self-righteous racist. The revival did not occur because he preached a great sermon. The words declared by a reluctant Jonah were only five Hebrew words — eight words when translated into English: "Yet forty days and Nineveh shall be overthrown" (Jonah 3:4).[48] Nor did the revival occur because of a religiously educated people group. The Ninevites were brutal idol worshippers. In no way was it the prophet, the preacher, or the people who brought a revival. The revival occurred because of the mercy of a loving God to an undeserving people.

The story of Jonah probably applies today more than any other book of the Bible in the context of American sentiments and mission. The setting for Jonah was Northern Israel during the days of the Assyrian Empire. The Assyrians had conquered much of the Fertile Crescent. Jonah lived in a tense political time for Jews. The Assyrians had pressured Israel militarily for years before Jonah's call by God. Although not an immediate threat at the time of Jonah, Assyrians later emerged as a powerful empire that claimed the northern territories of Israel.[49] Nineveh comprised part of the Assyrian Empire and, because of the political conflicts between the Assyrian Empire and Israel, Jonah hated the people of Nineveh.[50]

By all indications, Jonah was a patriotic Jew who loved his heritage, his people, and his homeland. By all historical accounts, Ninevites were brutal conquerors and had a deep neurotic bloodthirst unmatched by any ancient civilization of that day. Ancient ruins show carved scenes of them inflicting torture on their enemies. If the Ninevites had possessed YouTube capability, they no doubt would have posted videos of the torturous acts for the entire world to see. Jonah's patriotism collided with his enemy's violent nature and instigated a clash when Jonah received God's call to evangelize them.

Jonah ran from God's call — not out of fear, but out of hatred. He went to the port city of Joppa to set sail on a ship to Tarshish. Israelites considered Tarshish the farthest place on earth. Tarshish was a city to which God had not yet spoken a word, as affirmed in Isaiah 66:19.[51] Jonah went as far away from God's will as he possibly could by going to a place where he thought God would not speak to him. He felt by getting away, he could avoid God's call. This attitude still permeates some Christian minds today.

Many Christians in my circle talk about retiring from their jobs, selling out, and buying one hundred acres of land in the boondocks to get away from the world. But how can we fulfill the Great Commission when we live like a hermit in the middle of nowhere? I am not opposed to living in the country, but God never calls Christians to be hermits. He calls us to go to people with a message of mercy. Jonah looked for the boondocks when God wanted him to go to a city.

Jonah fled, but God sent a storm to reverse his course. When the storm hit the ship, Jonah told the sailors the storm was his punishment. They eventually threw Jonah into the sea. God then sent a great fish to swallow him. After three days in the belly of the fish, Jonah came to his senses. God spoke to the fish, causing it to vomit Jonah upon the shore. Jonah finally obeyed God and went to Nineveh.

Jonah preached one of the shortest and sorriest sermons in history. He merely declared Nineveh's doom and left. He did not call for a pianist to play endless verses of the invitation hymn, "Just as I Am." Jonah's abrupt sermon pointed to his hateful attitude toward the Ninevite people. He did not want them to repent. Despite Jonah's weaknesses, God brought a supernatural conviction upon the king of Nineveh and all its citizens. The great revival of Nineveh unfolded and even affected the animals of the city.

Chapter 4 displays the anger Jonah felt when God showed Nineveh mercy. Jonah ascended a high mountain to watch the city burn. When God removed His sentence from the people, Jonah gave God a piece of his mind.

> *Ah, Lord, was not this what I said when I was still in my country? … For I know that You are a gracious and merciful God, slow to anger and abundant in lovingkindness, One who relents from doing harm. Therefore now, O Lord, please take my life from me, for it is better for me to die than to live! (4:2-3).*

Jonah hated his enemies so much that he did not want God to forgive them. He wanted Nineveh to become a parking lot. His anger reached the point of pure ridiculousness when he asked God to end his life. I wish the story had a successful conclusion. I wish the story recorded Jonah coming to himself and truly learning what God was trying to teach him. But the story ends with Jonah remaining a jerk and God being gracious.

God said, "And should I not pity Nineveh, that great city, in which are more than one hundred and twenty thousand persons who cannot discern between their right hand and their left — and much livestock" (4:11).

God informed Jonah of a righteous reality: Jonah did not have the right to decide who should receive God's mercy. God saves and redeems whomever He chooses. We do not have the right to decide who can hear and receive the gospel. God decides who gets His loving mercy. Our role requires obedience to the calling of the Great Commission. Jonah, unfortunately, did not figure this out.

I wish I could say the Jonah syndrome does not exist today. We may think no one has this attitude toward his enemies and that the story of Jonah has no modern relevance. Nineveh is the modern-day city of Mosul, Iraq, and is the last stronghold of ISIS. Many probably feel the same way toward ISIS as Jonah did toward the Ninevites.

Before we point our fingers at Jonah, we should do some self-examination. What if God asked us to go to Mosul and share the gospel with the citizens of that godless city? Would we without debate get on a plane and go, or would we avoid that command like the plague? In my heart, God revealed the apathy I possessed toward people in Iraq.

People who live in Iraq are running for their lives from evil, and they need hope. We cannot all get on a plane and fly to Iraq tomorrow, but we can be honest before God and with ourselves about our feelings. Would we be happier if Jesus transformed the people of Mosul, or if He destroyed them? Our answer will determine whether we have the Jonah syndrome or the Jesus nature.

Nineveh is coming to us. The big cities and small communities of the United States are now dwelling places for people from ravaged Middle Eastern cities like Mosul and Damascus. God calls us to be His mouthpiece to them. The story of Jonah bids us learn from Jonah's mistakes and stand in awe of God's loving mercy.

God used this minor prophet's story to bring a turning point in my life and in my journey to engage Muslims with the gospel. Jesus addressed this issue in His Sermon on the Mount when He told us to love our enemies. Seeing the men and women of our armed forces die in battle is difficult, as is seeing those who survive return home without arms and legs and with PTSD. I see these realities among my circle of friends and in my church congregation. My heart breaks for them as I seek to shepherd them. But I also believe love will overcome evil, and that the gospel can transform the life of every nation.

Being a lover of my country like Jonah, I can fall into a bitter mode of hatred when I watch the news and see the evil head of ISIS emerge. Like the Ninevites, they revel in their ferocity, gleefully posting images of their brutality on YouTube for the entire world to see. At the same time, my patriotism cannot become an obstacle to my devotion to Jesus. My love for America cannot override my love for the kingdom of God. We must realize that not all Muslims belong to ISIS. ISIS has inflicted harm on just as many innocent Muslims as on Americans. It is not our job to "kill them all and let God sort them out." It is our job to proclaim Jesus to everyone and let God sort them out.

The story of Jonah illustrates the heart of patriotic people and their feelings toward their enemies. Patriotism is a good thing, but when it blinds us to loving our enemies, we become like Jonah. We will face Christian opposition if we befriend Muslims. They may treat us coldly. They may blast us on social media and call us traitors. When we face opposition from Christian friends over our befriending Muslims, we can point them to Jonah's story. He hated his enemies, but when he overcame his hatred, God brought wicked people to repentance.

As leaders who lead our churches to engage Muslims, the story of Jonah is a great place to start. Nineveh is an ancient symbol of the same region so many see as today's enemy. Jesus wants to save them. Be encouraged by Jonah's story.

Chapter 7

Look to the Unclean

When I get to heaven, I anticipate meeting the Apostle Peter. I think I will have to apologize for the hard time I have given him over the years in my sermons. I have dogged Peter for making dumb statements while talking to Jesus. Peter often spoke up too soon when Jesus posed a question and put his foot in his mouth by making fleshly statements. I have also heard sermons from other pastors who gave Peter a hard time — as if none of us would make dumb statements in the presence of perfection.

I remember being at the airport in Nashville, Tennessee, and seeing the famous country music band, Lonestar. I looked at them and said, "O my gosh, you guys are Lonestar!" They stared at me, seemingly stunned by the stupidity of the statement, as if to say, "Yeah, Captain Obvious." I am sure their response was a merciful version of what they thought. They simply said, "Yes, we are, and who are you?" I came to my senses and introduced myself.

I noticed we were taking the same flight, and I asked them where they were headed. They told me their destination, which happened to be the town next to where I lived. I told them where I was headed, and they asked me what I was doing that night.

"Nothing really. Just going home."

"Would you like to come to our concert and be our guest?"

"Absolutely."

"You can also get some backstage passes and come to our meet and greet."

"Absolutely."

The lead singer, Richie McDonald, pulled out his phone and asked, "How many tickets and passes do you need?"

I stammered and stuttered until I simply blurted out the number thirteen.

"Done," he said.

While on the plane, I told them their song, "Walking in Memphis," was my favorite song. And it still is. They turned out to be gracious people, and that evening was a great experience. I was able to take all four of my siblings and some friends to the concert. During the show, Richie McDonald said, "This next song is for our new friend, Josh, whom we met on Southwest Airlines today." They performed "Walking in Memphis" beautifully, and we all had a memorable night.

When I look back at how tongue-tied and foolish I was in the presence of a singing group, I must give Peter a break. I give Peter a hard time for saying dumb things to the Son of God, and I cannot even communicate with a country music band. With all that, I believe Peter is an awesome figure in Scripture. He is a man with whom I identify because he showed his flaws. However, Jesus transformed him.

When reading the journey of Peter in the Gospels, we see a man who boldly declared his love for Jesus in one instance but also denied knowing Him in other instances. Peter was a man of many contradictions and many inner struggles. Jesus called him Simon when he acted out in the flesh, but He called him Peter when he acted spiritually mature. Jesus even called him Simon Peter when he straddled the fence. Peter was a work in progress, but he eventually got it right. He finished strong and became a leader in the first-century church. Many can identify with his struggles.

Peter's struggles did not end in John 21 with the "feed my sheep" dialogue. He continued to work through his issues in the book of Acts. He displayed a glaring struggle that many Jewish Christians in the early church had to overcome: associating with Gentiles.

The Apostle Paul reports an account of Peter's struggle in his letter to the Galatians. In chapter 2, he speaks of a face-to-face confrontation with Peter that proved vital to Peter's spiritual growth. Peter shared a church meal with a group of Christian Gentiles in the city of Antioch. During the meal, James, the brother of Jesus and the pastor of the Jerusalem church, arrived. Peter responded by leaving the Gentile table because he feared Jewish backlash from James and the other Jews. His hypocrisy led even Barnabas the Encourager astray. Peter's actions hurt the Christian Gentiles serving in Antioch. Paul found this behavior so unacceptable that he confronted Peter publicly.

The divisions between Jews and Gentiles were not only unacceptable to Paul but also ungodly. Can anyone imagine a confrontation like this today? What if the head deacon saw the pastor snub someone at a church function, publicly rebuked the pastor in front of the church, and then posted the situation on social media for the sole purpose of making a spiritual point? Paul felt this intolerable behavior would damage the vitality of the gospel and the church. The fellowship and unity of all believers mattered enough for Paul to take drastic measures.

Luke records a series of events in the towns of Joppa and Caesarea that involved Peter and Gentiles. In Acts Chapter 10, Luke tells the story of Cornelius' conversion. Cornelius was a God-fearing Gentile who sought salvation, and God intervened to redeem him. God chose Peter to share the gospel with Cornelius. God did not use Paul, a man called to bear Jesus' name to the Gentiles. Rather, he chose Peter, the man who struggled with crossing ethnic and religious lines. God has a sense of humor.

Cornelius was a Roman centurion of Gentile roots, but a man who gave to the poor and prayed diligently to God. He was outside of the Christian circle but sought God. God came to him in a vision, telling him to find a man named Peter who was staying in Joppa. Peter would explain everything. Cornelius followed God's instruction and sent messengers to Joppa to locate Peter. The events led to the conversion of Cornelius and his entire family. God sent dreams and visions to both Cornelius the Gentile and Peter the Jewish Christian. Luke's account has many applications for breaking barriers so we can take the gospel into Muslim communities.

I believe God reveals Himself to Muslims through dreams and visions. Muslims believe the dreams of the faithful are prophetic. Common Muslims believe dreams are the only way to hear from Allah.[52] Many accounts reveal Muslims coming to Christ through dreams. Nabeel Qureshi wrote in his book, *Seeking Allah, Finding Jesus*, that dreams became one of the factors that drew him to faith in Jesus.

The account of Cornelius is like accounts recorded by missionaries in Muslim countries. Men like Nik Ripken and Kevin Greeson, author of *Camel Training Manual*, share many examples of God revealing Himself in dreams to bring Muslims to faith.[53] God uses dreams to draw people who are outside biblical influence, and, in this story, Luke recorded a prime example.

This is not only a reality in Muslim communities, but it also happens in other unreached people groups. I once went on a mission trip to Madagascar, an island the size of Texas situated off the southeastern coast of Africa. I spent several days backpacking through what Malagasy people call "the Red Island." A helicopter dropped us off and then picked us up later at a different region. We spent a total of nine days backpacking through the countryside, meeting and interviewing tribal leaders.

Visiting these regions of Madagascar was like a trip back in time. I saw no lions or zebras named Marty, but I did see lemurs and herds of cattle. We were met and guided by an IMB missionary named Kyle who led us through the bush for several days. He was a tremendous trailblazer for God on that island.

We came to gather cultural and religious data for the International Mission Board, which they would share with future church planters in the area. We entered villages and requested permission from the village elder to camp for the night. We then conducted interviews with different families, learning their cultural norms and religious taboos.

During one of the interview sessions, Kyle pointed to a hut on a remote hill and said, "Go to that hut. The village elders are waiting for you to interview them."

I took my interpreter, Epafra, with me. He was and is a great friend. By this time in our trip, we had already become good friends. He stood five feet, four inches tall and had more strength and energy than a man twice his size. He loved Jesus and enjoyed seeing God move. By this time, interviewing tribal elders was routine.

We entered the modest hut, which was like all others I had entered: mud walls, bulrush roof, bamboo trusses with dirt floors, and a fire pit in the corner to cook the daily meal of chicken and rice. The hut was packed with people, but they cleared a path for us.

I learned from Kyle in our briefings that we should always identify the elders of any group because these Malagasy tribes operated on an elder-led system. I recognized the elders in the room. Even with a language barrier, it only took a glance to figure out who was in charge. Two men who were twins and in their late fifties sat in the center of the room. This was the first set of twins I had seen in Madagascar. They were identical and bald. Their skin was black and worn from years of working cattle and laboring in the sun-beaten rice patties.

I bowed my head and shook their hands in respect, as previously instructed. I introduced myself and unloaded my routine speech. As I continued, one of the twin elders raised his calloused hand to stop me. He began talking in Malagasy tongue, and I listened intently. I watched Epafra and waited for the translation.

The others looked concerned and nodded their heads as he spoke. They looked at him and then looked at me as if the words of this man mattered deeply. As I watched Epafra, his eyes widened, and I noticed an astonishing look. I got nervous. I had learned only to get nervous in foreign fields if the interpreter got nervous.

To my relief, Epafra smiled and said, "Josh, this has never happened to me before, but they have a message for you. The elder says he and his brother have been having a repeated dream for quite some time. They have dreamed that the Creator of the universe has a Son who was born. They do not know who the Son is, but they feel we have been sent to reveal who that Son is."

I was stunned and excited all at once. The table had been set for me already, and I explained the story of redemption to the entire tribe. They listened intently and never moved. I gave the clearest gospel message I had ever given.

When I finished, the twin elder spoke again. He said tearfully, "Thank you. It is now clear, and all things make sense." I had been warned by the missionaries that if an invitation was given to a Malagasy tribe, the whole village would say a sinner's prayer whether they believed in Jesus or not.

I did not lead them in a sinner's prayer, but I told them that if they wanted to follow Jesus, they needed to go off by themselves and follow Jesus through prayer. I explained it carefully, and I felt that if God was powerful enough to prepare them for my message before I arrived, He was powerful enough to close the deal when I left the village. I left them with the gospel and a clear path to Christ. My experience in Madagascar comes to mind every time I read about Peter and Cornelius.

The vision given to Cornelius prepared the way for Peter to connect the dots. This leads to another applicable aspect of the story. As God used me to explain the gospel following a dream, so God used Peter to share the message following Cornelius' dream. God sent the vision to lead Cornelius to Peter, but God sent Peter to lead Cornelius to faith.

Why did God tell Cornelius to seek Peter instead of telling Cornelius the gospel message Himself? God wants His disciples to deliver the gospel. God does not open the clouds and audibly reveal the gospel. He does not use angels. He does not write it in the clouds. He uses His followers to declare the message of salvation.

God did not even use Paul, perhaps the obvious choice, to convert Cornelius. God chose Peter to deliver the good news. Perhaps God wanted to show readers of all times the beauty of breaking ethnic barriers with the gospel. Maybe this encounter was just as important for Peter's growth in understanding the character of God as it was for Cornelius to follow God.

Following Cornelius's dream in Caesarea, the story continued in Joppa. Peter visited a friend there and, as the family prepared a meal for him, Peter went on the roof to nap. During his sleep, he had a vision of a large sheet filled with unclean animals, descending from heaven. The Lord told Peter to kill and eat the animals, but Peter refused, telling God the animals were unclean (Acts 10:13-14).

As a faithful Jew, Peter abstained from eating unclean animals, which was commanded in the Levitical law.[54] God told Peter He had cleansed the animals. God was speaking about more than diets. He was lifting the barrier between Jew and Gentile.[55] God wanted Peter to understand this truth. Peter saw the vision three times, and God made certain it soaked into Peter's mind. Peter awoke from the trance and was met at the door by three emissaries from Cornelius's household.

Peter traveled to Cornelius's home and crossed the threshold. Jewish law forbade crossing this threshold, but God wanted Peter to cross this barrier. God used Peter, a man who struggled with Gentiles, to take a monumental step in saving the Gentile world. This event is momentous on so many levels.[56] Peter's statements regarding all that God had shown him speak volumes. He began his sermon by stating that he now understood that God shows no partiality (Acts 10:34). Peter understood God wanted all people to hear the message of salvation.

Because of Peter's obedience and the Holy Spirit's power, this whole Gentile household believed in Jesus Christ. As we read the rest of Acts, we can see how the gospel transitioned to the Gentile world. God was on the move to break ethnic barriers.

This story has similar markings as the Jonah story in the Old Testament. Jonah traveled to Joppa to avoid God's command to go to Nineveh. Peter was in Joppa on a tanner's roof when he received the vision from God. Peter's name was Simon Bar-Jonah, translated Simon son of Jonah. God commanded Jonah to go to the enemies of Israel (Nineveh) to share a message of repentance. God led Peter to the house of Cornelius, a Roman soldier. Roman soldiers symbolized the great opposition of first-century Palestine. Jonah did not want to obey God's call. Peter initially refused to kill and eat unclean animals. The resistance was prevalent in both accounts.

The similarities in both stories point to one clear message: God wanted to give His enemies a message of mercy. God used a man of God to speak for Him and deliver the message. God supernaturally got involved in both cases to complete His will. In both instances, Gentiles came to faith in God.

How does this relate to Muslims in America? In my own experience and my social circles, going to a Muslim's house and sitting for a meal was unthinkable. As a young Christian, it never entered my mind to dialogue with Muslims in any way. This was not even on my radar until God opened my eyes to Nineveh in America and the Cornelius's in my community.

I remember the first time I ate with a Muslim. It was like crossing an ethnic threshold, just as Peter did in Acts 10. I have also seen God do amazing things when I was willing to cross a Muslim threshold. If I can do it, anyone can. It started for Peter on a roof in Joppa. It started for me on a northbound highway in North Carolina.

We learn from Peter and Cornelius three life-changing truths. First, when the Holy Spirit leads us, ethnic barriers come down. In America today, we need this liberation more than ever. The Holy Spirit leads all communities to become gospel communities. Peter crossed a new threshold literally at Cornelius' doorstep and figuratively in history. We should pray and ask the Spirit to bring people together through our obedience. God will enable us to cross thresholds.

Second, when we follow God's direction, He usually leads us to uncomfortable places. Faith is stretched when God gets involved. We should pray and ask God to stretch our faith in this way. The greatest spiritual growth of our lives will occur when we venture into new cultures and new communities with the gospel.

Third, God will expand our family network. Our eyes have yet to see what God wants to show us on our journey with Him. Peter had no idea where God was leading him. If we follow the Spirit of God in crossing ethnic thresholds, we will one day look around and laugh for joy, realizing how far God has brought us. We can enjoy the expansion of territory in our lives when we obey His leading.

CHAPTER 8

LOOK BEYOND THE WALL OF PARTITION

I am an avid reader of biographies, history books, spiritual books, and books on about anything that interests me. My close friends found it amusing that I read *How I Helped O.J. Get Away with Murder* by Michael Gilbert, *The Screwtape Letters* by C.S. Lewis, and *Radical* by David Platt all in one winter.

I also read a book by Thom and Jess Rainer entitled *The Millennials*. This book is an eye-opening account of their research among millennials from all over the United States. The book covers numerous aspects of this generation of 78 million — the largest in our nation's history. I enjoyed the book because I consider myself a millennial in the brain, although I missed being born one by three months.[57]

Born in October 1979, I belong to Generation X by birth, but all the markings of the millennial generation are in my upbringing. I, too, witnessed the evolution from Atari to online gaming in my lifetime. I have placed phone calls from both a phone booth and an iPhone. I also enjoyed the book because I wanted a better understanding of millennials who I plan to pastor for the next thirty years and beyond.

One aspect of the research gave me hope for the future of Muslim evangelism. Millennials see racial diversity as a norm. Interracial marriage, interracial friendships, and societal diversity are such common realities to millennials that they do not understand why racism is such a polarizing social issue. Racial tensions still boil over in many communities of our nation, and millennials are not naive to these realities. Nevertheless, if the Rainer research is correct, the millennial generation do not consider people's skin color a factor in judging the value of their identity.

These opinions give a glimmer of hope that one day in America there will be peace between the races and religions. Racism remains a worldwide dividing tool of Satan and has throughout history. As Christ came to unite people with God and others, Satan works to divide and conquer. When people sit together at a table, unity eventually happens. Isolation and separation feed division, but when people unite, problems are resolved and peace is achieved. Nations develop diplomacy because agreements are reached when enemies look each other in the eye and talk through the issues.

The political situation in America is so divided because we lack meaningful, civil dialogue between the powers. All discourse is shouted from one side of the aisle to the other in news sound bites and social media posts. We need to resolve many issues, but division reigns because leaders will not come together. The problems of our nation and world will never be solved by social media messages. We need face-to-face dialogue.

Racism is one layer of division Satan uses in every culture. I once traveled to Quito, Ecuador, and witnessed the way the Ecuadorian government treated Quechuan Indians as lower-class citizens. Quechuans were not permitted to ride on standard public transportation, and the buses designated for them were limited.

I hiked into some of the most remote regions while in Madagascar and found tribal divisions. As I talked with tribes, they spoke of how worthless neighboring tribes were and of how they would not associate with them. From the eyes of an outsider, they looked the same. They ate the same foods, adopted the same ancestral worship practices, lived in the same reed huts, and lived by many of the same moral taboos, but they were divided in many ways.

Who can forget the religious division between Irish Catholics and Protestants? The conflicts were so violent in the 1990s that President Clinton traveled to Ireland to conduct peace talks. The Irish flag has three stripes — white, orange, and green — to symbolize the rift.

Even in the Appalachian Mountains, historical divisions exist between families and clans. Who can forget the Hatfield and McCoy feud of the late 1800s? My wife's extended family lives in the western Blue Ridge Mountains of North Carolina.

My wife and I vacationed in Andrews, North Carolina, one summer to attend her family reunion. I remember sitting on her great-grandfather's front porch, surrounded by beautiful mountains. I loved talking to her great-grandfather and listening to his stories. We called him "Paw Postell." He was ninety-six at the time but still had a sharp mind. He told me amazing accounts of his childhood and early life growing up in the mountains.

He once told me of his courtship with his late wife, Grace, my wife's great-grandmother. His parents were upset when he married her because she was from a different "holler." For those unfamiliar with Southern jargon, a holler is a small valley surrounded by hills. Back then, a person did not marry outside of their holler. The couple married in secret before they worked up the courage to tell everyone. They were married for sixty-seven years. I chuckle today when I think about that. They all went to the same churches, worshipped the same God, ate the same deep-fried cooking, and fished in the same fishing holes — but looked down on the people from the other holler.

Still today in America, the racial divide remains the stench that plagues us. Everyone has an opinion on these divisive and paralyzing issues, but Satan is winning the war in many places. However, God is on the move to counter these satanic strategies. He has been up to something powerful for centuries.

Although Satan strategizes to divide, Jesus came to unite. God aspired to bring the nations together in Christ through the gospel. The entirety of the Scriptures reveals this. As I studied the Scriptures anew, I saw this for the first time.

In Genesis 11, the story of the Tower of Babel shows God using language barriers to scatter the nations. King Nimrod unified the people to build a tower to heaven. God came down, stopped the project, and confused the languages. The nations then migrated because of their language barriers, and diverse cultures evolved over the centuries. In Acts 2, the opposite occurred. Pentecost was God coming down to lift the language barriers. As Peter stood and preached the gospel, God brought unity to those from diverse countries. God is still on a mission to bring the nations together under the cloak of the gospel.

The Scriptures reveal the heart of God to one day bring the Gentiles into His loving arms. Moses says in Deuteronomy 10:17-19 that God shows no partiality. He commands Israel to extend hospitality to the stranger, to feed them, to clothe them, and to love them. God wanted a hospitable hand from the Hebrew to the Gentile.

Leviticus 19:33-34, 24:22, Numbers 15:29, and Ezekiel 47:22 all similarly reiterate extending love to foreigners and sharing God's inheritance with them. Isaiah wrote, "The Lord God, who gathers the outcasts of Israel, says, 'Yet I will gather to him others besides those who are gathered to him'" (56:8).

God sought to gather others to Himself in the ages to follow. Pentecost was the start of the great harvest in every corner of the world. Many in attendance at Pentecost were practicing Jews from different nations, but God started with the house of Israel and extended the hand of grace to the Gentiles from the early church in Jerusalem.

Page after page, chapter after chapter, and book after book show the gradual unification between God and the nations. In the New Testament, the Great Commission was intended to go to the nations and, in the early church, we see the emphasis shifting to the Gentiles. Luke records the great revival in Samaria (Acts 8), followed by the conversion of the

Ethiopian eunuch along the roadside of the Gaza Desert. He then records the conversion of Saul in Acts 9 and the specific calling for him to take the gospel to the Gentiles.

Luke recorded the conversion of Cornelius in Acts 10, an incident that followed the vision delivered to Simon Peter in Joppa. Acts 11 describes the "church business meeting" where Peter was summoned to explain his reasons for entering Cornelius's house. Acts 15 describes James and all the elders resolving the issues of Gentiles and circumcision. We read of the Jewish struggle with the Gentiles receiving the gospel and what that meant for the Jewish culture. This was an issue in the Jewish culture, as well as in the days of Jesus and the early church. Luke chronicles these conflicts in many instances in the book of Acts. The domino events show God slowly but surely bringing the Gentiles into the family of God and unfolding His will of unity.

Who can forget the church in Antioch becoming the great launching pad to evangelize the Greco Roman regions of Asia Minor? Or the Macedonian vision revealed to the Apostle Paul in Troas, telling him to cross into Gentile lands with the gospel?

In Acts 17:26-27, Paul, summarizing God's love for all humanity, told his Athenian listeners, "And He has made from one blood every nation of men to dwell on all the face of the earth, and has determined their preappointed times and the boundaries of their dwellings, so that they should seek the Lord, in the hope that they might grope for Him and find Him, though He is not far from each one of us."

In his epistles, Paul emphasized the gospel's impact on all humanity. In his great treatise to the Romans, he illustrated his unwavering devotion to his fellow Jews — but in Romans 11, he described how God had grafted some new branches into the family tree of God: Gentile branches.

In his letter to the Galatians, Paul told them that everyone is a child of God who comes by faith in Christ Jesus. There is neither Jew nor Greek, and those in Christ are His heirs according to the promises (Galatians 3:26-29). Paul said the same thing to the church of Colossae (Colossians

3:11). In both of these instances, Paul reinforced that the gospel does not discriminate and is for all people who seek deliverance.

In his letter to the Ephesians, Paul eloquently described the moving reality that we were all aliens and strangers from God with no hope and no future apart from Christ. Jesus' blood, however, draws us close to God. Jesus has torn down the middle wall of partition. He has made peace and reconciled us through His death on the cross (Ephesians 2:11-22).

I realize now more than ever that seeing my Muslim neighbors as strangers and aliens is not acceptable to God. God has called His church to extend the hand of friendship to those far off. God is not okay with them being separated from Him, and neither should His churches. God shed His blood for them, and we are to take the gospel to them. God is in the unification business, and we should be as well.

I hope that God shows us all that we need to see the world through the eyes of Jesus, Paul, and Peter. If God wanted the Jews to take the gospel to Gentiles, then surely He wants a Gentile to take the gospel to other Gentiles. The wall of partition has been torn down. Let's not put it back up.

How do we take the wall down? We must stop being color blind. I hear well-intentioned friends make disturbing statements such as "God is color blind." Or "We should not see race when we see a person." I disagree. God is not color blind, and neither should we be. God made me a particular race, and when I look in the mirror, I see my race. This is God's design for me, and I am happy with that. God gets glory in color. He is not a bland artist. God is creative and created the human race with many colors.

We do not help race relations when we deny the color of creation. We take walls down by seeing others as God sees them and bringing them into the family through sharing Christ with them. Let's look beyond the wall and see in living color.

Section 3

Chapter 9

Look to Apply

Knowledge is power, but knowledge is powerless if not applied in daily life. Knowledge tells me that antifreeze keeps my car warm on winter days, but I apply that knowledge by putting it in the expansion tank of my car. Knowledge says antifreeze is a toxic poison, but wise application keeps me from putting it in my coffee as a sweetener. Maybe those are silly examples, but the application is necessary to make knowledge worthwhile.

I believe a sermon is not a sermon if it does not present application. What good is an eloquent message if people leave not knowing how to apply what they heard? American Christians do not suffer from a lack of biblical knowledge. Books on theological doctrines are at our fingertips. We can hear an infinite number of sermons on the web that teach us truth and biblical knowledge. Information is everywhere, but the application is scarce. Application equals success.

When I observed my surroundings, I found Nineveh surrounding me. I researched statistics and learned of Muslims coming to my part of the world. I studied the Bible and saw God's merciful hand extended to all nations and, in this case, my Muslim neighbors. But all I have learned means nothing unless I apply it.

I began engaging Muslims with the gospel several years ago, and I am still amazed at how God puts me at the table with them each week. I simply knocked on the symbolic Muslim door, and God pushed it open.

I discovered that Muslims heavily populated urban cities a short drive from my home. I prayed for courage and strength to engage them. I also researched Islamic religion and culture so I could communicate. I read books on the Muslim religion, traditions, and cultural values. I read books by former Muslims who are now followers of Christ. I read books by Muslim experts in missions and evangelism.

God caused my path to cross with many who were knowledgeable in doing mission work with Muslims. I absorbed their counsel and advice on various topics. They recommended books and resources, and I researched those pathways. I purchased an Aramaic vocabulary book so I could learn how to say "Hello," "Good morning," "What is your name," and other common phrases if I met a Muslim who did not know English. I became a student of their culture and pursued this people group — and all without setting foot on an airplane.

My pursuits did not become obsessions. I lived life as usual — taking my kids to school, coaching basketball, pastoring my church, and living a normal life. At the same time, I intentionally engaged them. As a result, I have enjoyed wonderful experiences.

One of my seminary professors, Dr. Joel Rainey, shared my passion and had many close friendships with Turkish Muslims. Because of my connection him, my wife and I received an invitation to celebrate Ramadan with some of his Turkish friends in Washington, D.C. Jaclyn and I jumped at the chance to go. By now, the Muslim evangelism bug had bitten my wife, too.

We drove to our nation's capital and rode the elevator to an upstairs business office in the heart of Washington's tourist district. We entered to a beautiful table prepared for our arrival. That evening, we feasted and fellowshipped with the participants and learned a lot about Muslims and their traditions. We experienced their welcoming hospitality. Dr. Rainey and his wife, Amy, were wise that evening. We followed their lead and came back with a new understanding of a world I had never experienced.

We listened as Dr. Rainey engaged in a basic yet polite theological discussion. These were not offensive and abrasive but respectful declarations of Jesus that our hosts were willing to hear. I noticed the importance of wisdom and going with the flow of the conversation when having theological discussions. Both Muslims and Christians left the table that evening with mutual respect for one another and a healthy knowledge of the gospel. I learned two important truths that night. First, I can engage Muslims just as my friends did. Second, the Turkish dessert, baklava, is heaven.

Our Ramadan encounter led to another experience I did not expect. Many of my professor's Turkish friends were interested in early American history and had mentioned they wanted to visit the Gettysburg Battlefield. Dr. Rainey knew my background in history. (I wrote my bachelor's thesis on the Battle of Gettysburg, I conducted tours of the battlefield for students in my teaching days, and I periodically took friends to the battlefield.) Dr. Rainey knew I was willing to give a tour and that I worked cheap, so he made the arrangements.

Over the following weeks, I met Turkish Muslim men at Gettysburg and gave them the grand tour. I took them to Devil's Den, Little Round Top, the cemetery, and all the highlighted spots of the sacred park. I was amazed by their knowledge of the Civil War and all that transpired in America's early history. They were more knowledgeable than most Americans I had guided.

Something happened at Gettysburg that rarely happens. I got lost driving around on the battlefield. I had traveled by car and horseback on that battlefield for an entire decade, and I had never gotten lost, but that day God had a plan.

This became a God-ordained course. In my detour, I had a deep conversation with three of my Muslim passengers. They knew I was a pastor and that I knew the Bible. They asked me questions about my faith. I had known this day would come, and I thought I was prepared for the typical questions: Why do you believe Jesus is the Son of God? How can you believe in a triune God? Do you believe Jesus died on the cross and rose from the grave? How do you know the Bible is reliable?

These were common questions I anticipated. But then they asked me if I believed in the rapture of the church. This question caught me off guard. Although I knew the rapture debate was prevalent in Christian circles, I never thought a Muslim would ask me that question.

I stammered and stuttered with my answer and then took the conversation further. I asked them a question: "Can I tell you how I became a Christian?"

"You were born a Christian right?" they asked.

"No, born again!" I said and then told them my testimony. I was a nine-year-old boy when I heard God call me in my mind to surrender my life and follow Him. At first, I told God no, but He pursued me for months. Then one night, I knelt at a church altar, repented of my sins, and placed my faith in Jesus. Once my prayer was finished, I stood, and I have been at peace with God ever since. I was born spiritually that day, and that is how I became a Christian.

One of the men asked, "Did God speak to you?"

"Yes, He did in my heart and mind."

He then asked, "Do you believe God speaks to all people?"

To keep the conversation simple, I answered, "Yes!" I then said that Jesus died for me and you, and if you surrender to Jesus, you will be saved.

He asked, "You have peace with God?"

"Absolutely, and I know that if I died today, I would be with God forever."

The van became deadly silent, and I thought I had blown it. I held my breath, and then one of my passengers responded, "I wish I could have peace."

I responded, "Through Jesus, all can have peace."

We finally found our way back on course. I was stunned by the speed of that conversation, but I did not want to push too hard. I believe God was in the van that day. He guided me off course to direct some Muslims on course. We had a great day, and, as we parted ways at the end of the day, the Muslim men hugged me. One, in particular, looked me in the eyes and said, "Brother, you have blessed three men today."

I responded, "I hope so, brother. *Salaam Alaikum*."

I have not seen those men since that day, but I learned that God's Spirit will move when we put ourselves out there for His purposes. I pray that our conversation will lead them to Christ. I do the natural, and Jesus does the supernatural. That day I did what I felt was natural. I talked about the Civil War and shared my testimony. God did the rest.

I have had many conversations like that during the past several years. At gas stations, coffee shops, hospitals, and dinner tables. The more faithful I am in engaging Muslims, the more God brings them to my doorstep. I look for opportunities and God simply delivers.

Engaging Muslims is easier than I thought because Muslims are open to talking about theology and religion. Talking theology and politics at a table together is culturally accepted, unlike in American culture.

Sharing our faith is as simple as being nice. An extended hand and a warm smile go a long way. All people desire friendship and hospitality. Hospitality is important in Muslim culture. Ninety-nine percent of encounters I have experienced have been positive. They want to show kindness because hospitality remains a major part of their cultural DNA.

I enjoy these meals and coffee breaks with Muslims so much that I long for other Christians to experience the feeling of engaging a new culture with the love, joy, and peace of Jesus. This is ministry, and this is the Great Commission.

In an Evangelism 101 class, students are instructed to witness this way. Many methods exist to engage people with the gospel, but one-on-one friendships work best. Relational evangelism is the most effective way to win people to Christ. This is true not only in Middle Eastern cultures but also in any culture. When we cultivate friendships, we cultivate an environment to share Jesus. Earning others' respect leads to a hearing. When we win their hearts, God will use us to win their souls. Satan does not want us to get together, but if Christians and Muslims sit at the same table and talk theology, the gospel truth will eventually prevail.

I have learned if I apply what I know, God will bless my efforts. There will be disagreements and discouragements. Days will come when we share our story and nothing seems to penetrate, but we can lie our heads down at night, knowing we were faithful to the Great Commission. When we take Jesus to places we never dreamed of, we see God the most.

Chapter 10

Look at My Tribe

I have asked God why He burdened me to reach Muslims. I am the most unlikely candidate. I speak with a southern drawl, even though I did not live in the Deep South when God gave me the burden. Although I lived in a state not considered in "Dixie," my home community at the time had many elements of southern living.

I lived in a rural conservative farm community. By no means did I see the realities of this community as negative. I love country life, and I loved that community. The people were simple and solid, and it was a great place to raise a family and serve Jesus. I drove to my church every day and saw farm silos on the horizon and corn combines working in the fields. When the wind shifted just right, I could smell the local mushroom farm, and I commonly heard roosters crowing at sunrise.

Most families spent their summer weekends at Little League fields and their fall weekends on soccer and football fields. Everybody knew everybody — and their business. It was a typical all-American community with all its warts. The community, however, had a dark past: a racist dark streak. My hometown had been known as a hub for Ku Klux Klan activity.

Fortunately, the county has moved away from those sentiments. The county is still predominantly Caucasian but has become more diverse. Most who live and work in the community want to distance themselves from their past and create a new community of peace and diversity.

The town was only a short drive from several major US cities. I could enjoy rural life but be where the action was in thirty minutes. Still, the community was the least likely place to become a bastion of Muslim evangelism.

The church I pastored was founded in 1954, averaged six hundred in weekly attendance, and had seen steady growth. They had two worship services on Sunday morning. We called our music blended, but I called it traditional contemporary. They sang songs by Chris Tomlin, Jeremy Camp, Dave Crowder, and other contemporary artists of the day, but they still cherished the old hymns like "Amazing Grace," "How Great Thou Art," and "I'll Fly Away." The church choir still wore robes and sang Brooklyn Tabernacle favorites. We still had Sunday school and Sunday evening worship services.

Seventy percent of the members were under fifty. We had millennials worshipping with baby boomers, as well as those from the greatest generation. The nurseries and junior church ministries were full, and the Awana ministry was a big hit on Wednesday nights. The youth ministry was also healthy.

The campus boasted forty-four acres with a gorgeous worship center containing wooden pews, a wooden cross pulpit, beautiful lobbies, and great technology. They enjoyed a great website and a terrific cohesive staff. They had a healthy budget with many generous givers and loving donors to Great Commission causes.

We averaged thirty baptisms every year. The church gave to mission work in selected places where they chose to make a long-term investment. By Baptist measurements, the church was successful. They had the "Three Bs": buildings that were state of the art, baptisms that were steady, and a healthy budget. People were saved and disciples were made. They hoped one day to do some church planting.

The church personality modeled the community, with blue-collar workers, former military men and women working in government contracting positions at a nearby military base, farmers, police officers, nurses, and schoolteachers. The members hunted and fished for leisure, coached sports, and raised their families.

My tribe proudly claimed the title of "Redneck." Jacked-up trucks, Real Tree camouflage jackets, and NRA stickers were commonplace. To be called a redneck was a badge of honor. Some of our most popular events were turkey shoots at Thanksgiving and wild game suppers in the late winter. It was not unusual to hear conversations about Donald Trump and Making America Great Again. It was also common to hear claims of boycotting the NFL due to players' refusal to honor the National Anthem.

What God did to use my community and church to reach Muslims was important, mainly because my church was typical in many respects. Church's personalities are unique, but we hold to common evangelical doctrines. Some churches may not be as healthy, and some may be much healthier, but ours was a typical Southern Baptist church following Baptist doctrine and supporting Baptist mission organizations. They held to the Baptist Faith and Message and gave faithfully to Cooperative Program partnerships. Although I serve in a different church now, that was my tribe at one phase of my journey — my redneck tribe. Everyone has a tribe, and we seem to stay in our tribe. I looked at my tribe and wondered if they would be willing to reach people outside their boundaries. I wondered if rednecks and Muslims could mix.

Chapter 11

Looking to Lead

When God began working on my heart and bringing Muslims into my life, I wanted my congregation to see what I saw. I wanted them to engage Muslims also.

Showing compassion to Muslims would be a difficult obstacle. My church was pro-military, pro-Israel, conservative, and traditional. How would I convince a church with those convictions to love those whom they considered their enemies?

When I attended my first Ramadan feast, I asked permission from the church leadership because I feared the backlash it might create. They gave me their blessing. When some of my fellow church members heard I was taking Turkish Muslims to Gettysburg, they shared their concerns for my safety. They promised to pray for me. God intervened in my situation and spoke to their hearts.

I saturated my burden in prayer and asked God to give me the wisdom to lead our church. I went to the senior pastor — my father — and shared what I believed was an excellent opportunity. If I were going to lead our church to engage Muslims, I needed his blessing. Keep in mind that he was the man at the White House on 9/11. Having experienced a portion of that tragic day firsthand, I anticipated he would resist my idea.

I shared my heart and all God had shown me. Amazingly, he had been seeing and experiencing the same epiphanies. He had recently returned from Israel and, on his trip, had gone through Jordan to visit the tourist sites at Petra. He had shared his faith with a Jordanian merchant selling souvenirs. The encounter made his evangelistic wheels turn in Muslim directions. We prayed for God to reveal the next step and how to lead our church. We then shared our burdens in the next deacon's meeting. They listened and nodded their heads, but no one said anything. Everything said seemed of little importance at the time.

A few weeks after our conversation, one of our deacons told us about an Egyptian man whom he had met at work. This man, whom I will call Ader, had served in Jordan for twenty years as a pastor for Campus Crusade for Christ. This grabbed our attention. He and his family had immigrated to the United States to seek medical treatment for one of his children.

We arranged a meeting with Ader and began cultivating a relationship. He and his family spoke fluent Aramaic and were rather fluent in English. They were born-again believers and shared our burden to reach Muslims in America. God supernaturally merged our lives, and I found reassurance that God was up to something great.

While the friendship with Ader and his family grew, I took every opportunity to communicate to our congregation the need to see our Muslim neighbors as a field of harvest. That communication started in the pulpit when I preached.

I preached about the Angel of the Lord's promise to Hagar and Ishmael. I shared about God's plan for Ishmael and Isaac's children. I preached about Jonah and how God had called him to evangelize his enemies. I showed the congregation the connection between Nineveh and Mosul, and how we are called to love our enemies. A sermon I entitled "The Jonah Syndrome" struck a chord with the members, and I saw God stirring hearts.

I preached about the Samaritan woman and communicated how Muslims were seeking water. I reminded them we carried Jesus' living water. I preached about Peter and Cornelius. I reminded them of how Jesus had torn down the wall of partition between all people groups. I spoke about the family reunion set at the throne of God in Revelation 7 and how every tribe and tongue will worship the Lamb of God in Heaven. For two years, I preached.

These sermons invoked dialogue among our people. Church reaction varied. Some became more interested in reaching Muslims. Some absorbed these sermons with a new unction. A few became agitated. I dialogued with our people one on one. I answered their questions to the best of my ability and tried to prepare them to see the opportunities. Slowly, people caught the fever.

I scheduled expert speakers to preach and direct seminars to open the congregation's eyes to Muslims' needs around the world. I also called on some friends to help me equip my church family. Nik and Ruth Ripken assisted in our church's learning process.

My wife, Jaclyn, called on Ruth Ripken to help our women's ministry leaders learn about engaging Muslim women. Our women's ministry hosted a Middle Eastern banquet. The women decorated the fellowship hall with Middle Eastern decorations, prepared Middle Eastern foods, and sat on the floor in Middle Eastern style to dine together. The event was a success and helped our women see evangelism through fresh eyes. The banquet became a pivotal night for future Muslim ministries and created a comfort level for our women.

Several months later, Nik and Ruth Ripken came for an entire weekend and preached on Christian persecution and Muslim opportunities. We promoted the weekend for months and named the event, "Faith Afire Weekend." On Friday, 156 people attended the seminar. On Saturday, 256 attended, and on Sunday, 442 attended. I was ecstatic. The seminar was based on Nik's book, *The Insanity of God*.

By the end of the Sunday morning session, we could sense a change in the congregation's mood. Nik Ripken approached me and whispered, "The Spirit is heavy in here, and He is about to break through. Be ready for the altar to be covered." He was right. By the end of the next session, many in the congregation wept. Nik gave an altar call, and people filled our altar. I prayed with those seeking my assistance.

Later, many told me what God had shown them. Many sought God's forgiveness for not loving their enemies. Many confessed their sin of neglecting people and failing to share the gospel. Some even confessed their hatred of Muslims. Ripken's words also helped the congregation understand Islamic cultures and heightened their awareness of Muslims' need for the gospel. The Faith Afire Conference also served as a key component for our church to reach a new local people group. This seminar brought awareness, but the next seminar brought engagement and knowledge.

I dedicated our Sunday night services for the next eight weeks to receiving Muslim evangelism training via DVD. I ordered the Seeking Allah Finding Jesus video seminar and advertised it to the congregation for several weeks. We started the seminars on Super Bowl Sunday night. I did not realize the conflict until it was too late. I considered changing the starting week, but the busy church calendar left me no choice.

I drove to church that night, expecting to see only a few cars in the parking lot. What I saw stunned me. On Super Bowl Sunday night, we had 152 attend the session. We usually averaged around seventy-five on Sunday evening, but this night God and our congregation exceeded my expectations.

For the next eight Sunday nights, we averaged 120 people. The congregation got excited about what they were learning through the sermons and seminars. Members approached me, asking me to recommend books to help them learn about Muslim culture and the tenets of Islam so they could effectively communicate. Members also approached me with exciting stories.

A young woman named Nicole, who was a nurse, shared how she worked with a Muslim woman. She had always gotten along great with the woman but did not know enough about Islam to share her faith. She now had the gospel knowledge she needed.

Debbie, a retired nurse, looked out her window during this time to see her new neighbors. After meeting them, she discovered they were from

Iran. She developed a friendship with the woman and brought her to our church for various events. Her new friend came on one occasion to help the women sort Christmas gifts for our Angel Tree delivery ministry. We were all able to show her kindness. Debbie eventually witnessed to her.

One Sunday, Nick, the owner of a small lawn care business, approached me and told me his latest story. "Pastor, I have mowed grass for a Muslim gas station owner for years, but now for the first time, I shared the gospel with him."

These are just a few stories of how God opened doors for our church congregation as they looked around their community.

I underestimated my church family. I doubted they would extend a hand to Muslim Americans, but they proved me wrong. God prepared me to do Muslim outreach, and many in my church followed.

As we led and equipped the congregation, God brought Ader closer to our church family. We brainstormed and developed a strategy to reach Muslims in the closest major city where a major Muslim population lived. My initial idea was to plant a church in the area and have Ader serve as pastor. But Ader cautioned me that a church plant would repel rather than attract Muslims.

He suggested a community center approach, which he believed would have a greater impact. Community centers are common in Islamic cultures all over the world. Muslims go to local community centers for social interaction, coffee, and internet access.

We spent the next two years raising support and looking for a good location. We faced some adversity finding the right and affordable location, but we eventually settled at a storefront location in the heart of our target area. This area proved to be a godsend and the perfect location. We were down the street from the city library and across the street from an immigration resettlement center. Whenever an immigrant came to our city, they were directed to the immigration resettlement center. Ader went to the resettlement center and invited the people across the street for coffee and fellowship. This meant all immigrants from Muslim countries gravitated to our location to receive assistance.

As the ministry blossomed, we discovered needs that faced each family and offered services to meet those needs. These individuals came to America legally through the lottery system from Syria, Jordan, Egypt, Sudan, Iraq, and Afghanistan. The Syrian Civil War, the invasions of ISIS, and other turbulent disasters had displaced them.

They were grateful to be in America. Many of our volunteers and I developed a greater appreciation for America. I remember sharing a meal with a Syrian family. As we talked about their new life in America, I heard sirens blare in the background. The ringing of sirens was not uncommon since the city was one of the bloodiest and most violent in America.

I rolled my eyes and said, "I'll bet you get scared and tired of hearing these sirens every day."

"No. I love that sound because in America that means help is coming. In my country, there is no help coming. When you hear sirens, that means bombs are falling. Here you just dial 911, and people come to save you from danger."

Those statements gave me a different perspective on the blessings I enjoy every day. Though these refugees are poor, they are safe. The government provided some assistance for them to get on their feet, but their inability to speak our language made daily tasks difficult. Common routine matters for Americans constitute daunting challenges for them. Reading the mail, understanding apartment leases, buying cars, registering children for school, and scheduling doctor appointments were responsibilities that proved problematic because of language barriers.

We enlisted volunteers from our church, as well as other partnering churches, to teach English. We also recruited people to sort through their mail. Every day, Muslims came to the center with their recent mail. Our volunteers read the mail and helped explain the contents, throwing out the junk mail and explaining what was important. If phone calls were necessary, we made them and also mediated their medical, insurance, and motor vehicle matters.

The ministry grew beyond our expectations. We had clothing drives, Christmas parties, and Saturday boys' and girls' clubs. The center became the central location of the ministry. While we served these families, we developed relationships with them and had many gospel conversations. Interaction between those of my church and Muslims increased throughout our journey. Unexpected events unfolded as the ministry grew.

We went from serving five families to ten families. Then, in what seemed like a short period, we were working with forty families. We were overwhelmed by the doors God had kicked wide open.

Many in the congregation helped in different ways. Some of the men helped remodel the center by painting, installing appliances, and fitting the rooms for service. I remember one day looking at the construction team. All of them were former military men who had experienced Muslims as the enemy. Now, they prepared a building to reach them. I saw Matthew 5:44 in action that day: "But I say to you, love your enemies, bless those who curse you, do good to those who hate you, and pray for those who spitefully use you and persecute you."

Women from our church invited Muslim women to their homes and got to know them. The church found ways to meet their needs. We collected funds to buy gift cards during holiday seasons like Thanksgiving and Christmas. Giving gifts during these holidays allowed us to show the love of Jesus and share the gospel at the same time. One Muslim man asked about the origin of Thanksgiving and what the holiday meant. I used that opportunity to explain thankfulness to God for saving me from my sins.

I initially thought Muslims would never come to our church for anything. I discovered that they gleefully accepted our invitation to various events. Since the church was filled with hunters and outdoorsmen, one of the most popular events at the church was our Wild Game Feast. The hunters brought their harvested game from the year of hunting and loaded tables with venison, wild boar, Canadian geese, and elk. Some brought more exotic meats such as camel, possum, black bear, and muskrat.

Ader told me the Muslim men from the center wanted to attend the event. We welcomed them warmly. We labeled the meats because we knew our friends would not eat pork. They fellowshipped with our people and enjoyed the food and company. We brought in a guest speaker from our state convention. He presented the gospel, and the men listened intently while Ader translated.

Many of the donated prizes included ammunition, knives, slingshots, and gift cards to Bass Pro Shop and Cabelas. The grand prize was a crossbow. Each drawing for a weapon or ammo seemed to go to one of our guests. The looks on many of our church members' faces were priceless. Handing out ammo caused an uneasy feeling, but we appreciated the humor in the situation. The Muslims approached me afterward and returned the ammunition, saying they had no use for it.

I would never have imagined my church hosting a Wild Game Feast and sharing hunting gifts and the gospel with Muslims. God is good, and the Wild Game Feast was a surprising success. We learned two important facts about our friends that night. First, they were willing to come to our church for fellowship. Second, they loved to eat venison. Discovering that Muslims loved venison spurred a new aspect of our ministry. Many of the deer hunters donated processed deer to the Muslims at the center.

One of my friends from church, Duane, called me at the beginning of hunting season and told me God wanted him to donate his first deer of the season to the Muslim families. We delivered his first fruits that year to a Middle Eastern family.

I decided it was my turn to invite my new friends to my house for a cookout. My wife, Jaclyn, and I had wanted to open our home, but we had one obstacle: "Porkchop" lived next door. Porkchop was our neighbor's pet potbelly pig. He was a friendly little oinker that wandered freely and would randomly mosey over to our backyard and lounge in our barn. One day, I walked into the barn to grab something, and he squealed with that ear-piercing shriek that makes the teeth vibrate.

Our kids loved to pet and scratch Porkchop when he came over. I visualized a backyard full of Muslims with Porkchop running through the yard squealing and causing chaos. This would be a disaster that could dampen our effort to form relationships.

I told God (as if He needed me to make Him aware of things) that I could not have my friends over because of the pig next door. I gave the issue to Jesus and moved on. A few days after my conversation with Jesus, I looked out my window and into our neighbor's yard. I saw a backhoe digging a hole at the base of a tree. I walked over and asked what had happened.

"Porkchop died last night."

"What?"

"Yep, we went out this morning to feed him breakfast, and he was dead in his stall."

I am not saying God killed Porkchop. Part of me was heartbroken because my neighbors are amazing, and Porkchop was a sweet pig. But to this day, I am stunned by the timing.

With the death of Porkchop, my wife and I felt God had given us the green light to have a cookout with our friends. We set a date and sent out invitations. Forty Syrian Muslims of all ages came to our home on a hot July day for a backyard cookout.

I remember driving our church van to our house, loaded with fifteen Muslims who had never been outside the city. They were fascinated with the rows of corn and the livestock in the pastures. They had never experienced this aspect of American culture. When I arrived at the house, I found that others had arrived early. My wife and the women were inside cooking, and the Muslim women I brought joined them. The men stayed in the front yard under my shade trees, smoking cigarettes and conversing in Arabic. My rural country road had never seen a Syrian invasion like this. Our neighbors curiously gazed out their windows.

We have a swimming pool, and the teenage boys brought their

swimming trunks. I opened the gate but found out quickly that some could not swim. Two young boys did not know that the pool had a sloping drop from the shallow end to the deep end. Off they went into the deep end, flopping underwater. Some of us jumped in and pulled them out. I called Ader over and asked him to explain the depth of the pool. I could see the newspaper headline the next day: "Syrian Teenagers Drown in Baptist Pastor's Pool."

Other than the near-death of two young boys, the day went smoothly. My wife did an amazing job preparing food. I blessed the food, and we fed them grilled chicken and deer burgers with all the sides. They loved the desserts and popsicles.

We shared great conversations and learned more about their experiences. We talked about how they came to America. We talked about Islam and the differences in our religions. We finished the day with group photos and giving gifts. My church had prepared gift bags for each family. Each bag consisted of grocery store gift cards, lotions for the women, and an Arabic New Testament. We also gave bubbles and small toys to the children. At the end of that day, I felt as if I had been Jesus more than ever before. My wife and I experienced a feeling of accomplishment and fulfillment. Everyone in the church who helped experienced the same feeling.

The journey for me and the church started on a northbound highway. I followed the burden in my own life, but at the same time, God got involved. Although many in our congregation did not catch the passion I had for reaching Muslims, many more did. I am proud of how far the church went. They no longer fear Muslims or have any apprehensions about engaging them with compassion and truth. We overcame great milestones.

At the beginning of that journey, I wanted to lead the church to do something great, but I discovered that I simply had to follow the example of our Lord Jesus Christ. Jesus blazed this trail by coming to earth. We simply follow Him on this road.

Chapter 12

Look to the Future

Soren Kierkegaard once wrote, "Life can only be understood backward, but it must be lived forward."[58] This has been true with my Muslim ministry experiences. The past has been rewarding and challenging. My church family and I share many stories that demonstrate how God led us to reach our Muslim friends. I was only one member of a great team that made that ministry possible.

The center we founded thrived in the city. I went once a week to eat and fellowship with my Muslim friends. I served them by helping with their daily mail and teaching them English. I am now a student of the Arabic language because they taught me. Other volunteers also served at the center.

We helped them with their immigration papers and assisted them with getting jobs. Our goal was to see them receive full citizenship and find a livelihood to provide for their families. They wanted to enjoy the American dream, and I wanted them to enjoy the freedom I treasure. At the most, we prayed that they would become citizens of the kingdom of God and enjoy heavenly freedom for eternity.

We visited their homes regularly for coffee and lunch. They became dear friends. Eventually, Ader and his family reached one hundred Muslim families in the city. Our little two-room center became overcrowded. Other churches collaborated with us to accomplish the work. They lent their buildings and time to host ministry events. That ministry was without question a team effort that was bigger than I was.

In 2017, we witnessed our first conversion to Christ. A young Iraqi immigrant from Baghdad, whom I will call Wade, gave his life to Christ at the center. Wade was like many of the other Muslims we served. He moved to America to find a job and live the American dream. He visited our center to find assistance in finding a job. Soon, he began asking questions about Jesus and the Bible. Two weeks after Wade gave his life to Jesus, he was baptized at our church on Sunday morning. When Wade came out of the water, the church erupted in applause like never before.

We enjoyed many joyful moments, but the work was a daily grind. In the end, God saved sinners. We simply shared the love of Jesus and the message of the cross. We continued presenting the message as much as God allowed, believing God would bring a great harvest in the future.

I also believed that even if God had not redeemed one Muslim, we had done the right thing. We shared Jesus with Muslims because God commanded us. We share the gospel and live the gospel for God's glory, not because of the results. I pray for more of my Muslim friends to come to faith in Christ, but if they do not, we should still obey God's command.

We also faced financial, spiritual, cultural, and logistical challenges. Andy Stanley wrote, "Ministry is messy!"[59] I fully agree. We endured criticism from cynics and alienation from some Christians. Not everyone in the church got involved, but those who did not did not oppose it. Those who did invest did so with great delight. They bought into the vision, and many of them contributed heavily to the ministry. The church grew as they obeyed the Great Commission. Anyone can do what we did.

When the chaos in Afghanistan unfolded after US forces left, thousands of refugees fought to board US airplanes and evacuate the country. Two hundred refugees were sent to Dulles International Airport in Washington, D.C. Many of these refugees were displaced to Baltimore, and the ministry center was ready. Ader and countless volunteers pitched in and raised funds from all over the country to meet their needs. God used His people to be a light to hurting Muslims in need of Christ's love.

Jaclyn and I once traveled to St. Petersburg, Russia. We loved the history, the food, the palaces, and the museums. As a history buff, I was in heaven. One of our favorite stops was the Church of the Resurrection, also known as the Church of Savior on the Spilled Blood.

In 1881, Russian Tsar Alexander II was assassinated by a revolutionary's explosion. The church was built on the spot of his assassination. Like most tourists, we shopped in the marketplace. I was shocked to see Russian stacking dolls painted like Deshaun Watson and the players from the Clemson Tigers. I could not resist and bought a set. I am sure I was the only Clemson fan in Russia.

After satisfying my weaknesses, we went inside the church where I beheld one of the most beautiful sights I have ever seen. The interior walls were decorated with a magnificent mosaic from floor to ceiling that told the biblical account from creation to Revelation. All the famous scenes from Scripture were painted in picturesque colors. The tour guide said the tsars had funded the project to teach the Russian people the story of the Bible. Due to poor literacy, the people could not read the Bible in those days, so the tsars provided a way for the people to learn the redemptive story visually.

Each mosaic piece was one square inch. Thousands upon thousands of little square pieces made up the grand masterpiece. I could not help but think that I was just one small piece in God's grand story. All of us involved in reaching the nations for Christ are small pieces composing a grand story that God the author is unveiling one piece at a time.

Sometimes I wonder about the future of God's story. What part do American Christians and American Muslims play? Will He bring a revival to Muslims in America? This is happening in other nations. We pray for revival to come to our land. What if God does bring a revival in America? Could it be that the greatest revival in America will take place among the Muslim communities?

As in Nineveh, the greatest moves of God are sometimes in the most unlikely places. God seems to go where the religious people least expect. What if Christians and Muslims sat at the same table and had fellowship together? I believe the gospel will win. I believe a revival will happen. Satan knows that, and that is why he fights to divide.

What if churches in Nashville, Raleigh-Durham, Atlanta, Houston, Los Angeles, and Washington, D.C. decided to find ways to engage Muslims? What if suburban and rural churches across America sought out their Muslim neighbors? What if evangelical Christians collectively focused on this unreached community?

Churches do not have to start community centers and do ministry the way our church did. We can engage Muslims at work. Anyone can be friendly and carry on a friendly conversation.

What if Muslims saw Jesus in us? What if Muslims saw light in us? What if Muslims got a drink of living water from us? What if salt was applied in decaying places? This is God's heart. This is also the heart of Scripture and the Great Commission.

We will never lead Muslims to Jesus by ignoring or segregating them. We must show them hospitality and kindness just as Jesus showed us kindness. This is so important for the future of our nation and our churches. We do not have to go on short-term mission trips to discover them. All we must do is go to an American coffee shop, the local library, the grocery store, or a local park. If we seek them, we will find them.

Nineveh surrounds us. There would be no evangelized Samaritan woman if there had not been an engaging Savior. Like Jonah, we should engage Nineveh, but with a willing heart. May we be like Peter and engage Cornelius' house. May we contribute to the great reunion in heaven of every tribe and every tongue by engaging those nations. The wall of partition has been removed, and Jesus is telling us to go.

When I look to the future, I see God receiving all whom He paid for on the cross. I want to be a part of that grand mosaic. God lays different tribes on our hearts, but we should follow His leading. Roll up your sleeves and get dirty fulfilling the Great Commission. It is messy, but it is worth it. Look for those who are not like you and prayerfully engage them for the sake of the call.

Appendix

Key Steps to Personally Engage Your Nineveh:

01. Observe your surroundings and make note of ethnically diverse communities.
02. Take time to research the demographics of your community, city, and state.
03. Pray and seek God's wisdom for ways to engage those with whom He identifies.
04. Research their culture through books, documentaries, and online resources.
05. Study their religious beliefs and how they worship. Find the differences and similarities between Christianity and their religion.
06. Read books and watch video sources by experienced authors and missionaries who can teach you how to reach your group and share areas to avoid.
07. Intentionally go to places that the people group may frequent: restaurants, coffee shops, local businesses. Interact with them in a friendly conversation.
08. Build a friendly relationship and show kindness first. They are not test cases; they are people.
09. Let the relationship grow at its natural pace, and let gospel conversations evolve as the friendships grow. Trust must be established.
10. Exchange gifts, share meals, invite them to family functions if plausible and safe. Let them experience your culture. Go to their events and share in their culture.
11. When religious conversations happen, be ready to dialogue on

their level, but be honest. If you do not know the answer to their questions, admit it.
12. Ask them questions about their religion so they feel equal to you in the conversation.
13. If you do not know the answer to a challenging question, find it and bring it to them at another time.
14. Tell them the story of how you came to faith in Christ. Your testimony is your greatest weapon.
15. Let God do the supernatural. It may take years to win a person to Christ, especially if they are from another religious culture. Let it evolve through the Holy Spirit's conviction.
16. Watch the wonders God will do through your willingness and diligence.
17. Pray hard and watch God bring the harvest.

Key Steps to Lead Your Church to Engage Your Nineveh:

01. Pray and seek God's help.
02. If you are a church leader seeking to lead others in engagement, share your burdens, knowledge, and experience with the power players of the church.
03. If you are a layperson, share your burdens, knowledge, and experiences with your leaders, or at least with trustworthy friends.
04. Show in Scripture why reaching people is important.
05. Show the need in your community through data and observations.
06. Take your time; you cannot change people quickly.
07. If you are a pastor, preach a sermon series that relates to outreach and then show the urgency of the need.
08. As your team members and friends buy into the vision, provide avenues for them to learn how to connect (books, video seminars, conferences, internet video links).

09. Frequently share personal stories of how God used you in your journey.
10. See what God does and guide your church as the burdens cultivate and the opportunities present themselves.
11. Use the methods that work for your people. No two churches or organizations will use the same approach.
12. Pray hard, and let God bring the harvest.

Notes

Section 1

Chapter 2 — Look at Recent Decades

01. Pew Research Center. "World's Muslim Population Will Surpass Christians This Century." http://www.npr.org/sections/thetwo-way/2015/04/02/397042004/muslim.
02. The American Thinker. "The Muslim Population of America Is Expanding at Warp Speed." http://www.amercianthinker.com/articles/2015/01/the_muslim_population.
03. Muslim Academy of Language Culture and Religion. "Top Ten Muslim Cities in America." http://muslim-academy.com/top-ten-muslim-cities-in-america-2.
04. Texas Muslims. http://www.muslimpopulation.com/America/USA/Texas Musalmans.php.
05. Sabre Ahmad. "The Muslim Community of Georgia." http://aliman.wordpress.com/2006/10/05/the-muslim-community-of-Georgia.
06. Data provided by Muslim statistician Samir Abraham and his research.
07. Islamic Research Foundation International, Inc. "Muslims in Louisville." http://www.irfi.org/articles_101_150/muslims_in_louisville.html.
08. The New York Times. "Nashville's Latest Big Hit Could Be the City Itself." http://nyti.ms/UHgBFD.
09. Al Jazeera. "Immigrants Thrive in US Country Music Capital." https://www.aljazeera.com/features/2012/10/15/immigrants-thrive-in-us-country-music-capital.

10. Al Jazeera, "Immigrants."
11. Information collected from a 2017 article in USA Today.
12. David Garrison, *A Wind in the House of Islam* (Monument, CO: Wigtake Resources 2014), 37-39.
13. Garrison, *A Wind in the House of Islam*, 18.

Chapter 3 — Look at the Giants

14. Barna Research. "Is Evangelism Going Out of Style?" http://www.barna.com/research/is-evangelism-going-out-of-style.
15. Pew Research Center. "New Estimates Show US Muslims Population Continues to Grow." http://www.pewresearch.org/fact-tank/2018/01/03/new-estimates-show-US-Muslim-population-continues-to-grow.
16. Lifeway Research. "Most American Pastors Say Islam Is a Dangerous Religion." https://theaquilareport.com/lifeway-research-most-american-pastors-say-islam-is-a-dangerous-religion/.
17. Pew Research Center. "U.S. Muslims Concerned About Their Place in Society, but Continue to Believe in the American Dream." http://www.pewforum.org/2017/07/26/findings-from-pew-research-center.
18. Al Jazeera. "Fears Rife Within American Muslim Community after Chapel Hill Shootings." http://america.aljazeera.com/articles/2015/2/17/threats-to-muslim-americans.
19. Al Jazeera, "Chapel Hill Shootings."
20. Pew Research, "U.S. Muslims Concerned."
21. Rasmussen Reports. "Just 17% Believe American Muslims Are Treated Unfairly." http://www.rasmussenreports.com/public_content/politics/general.
22. Lisa Cannon Green. Lifeway Research. "Americans Sure of Religious Freedom but Unsure Muslims Are Welcome." http://lifewayresearch.com/2015/07/29/americans-sure-of-religious-freedom-but-unsure-muslims-are-welcome.

23. Lifeway Research. "Most Pastors Say Islam Is A Dangerous Religion."
24. Nabeel Qureshi. *Understanding Jihad*. (Grand Rapids: Zondervan, 2016), 91.
25. Qureshi, *Understanding Jihad*, 77.
26. John Esposito. *The Future of Islam*. (Oxford University Press, 2010), 30.
27. J.D. Greear. *Breaking the Islam Code*.
28. Christopher Wright. *The Mission of God*. (Downers Grove, IL: InterVarsity, 2006), 45-46.
29. Wright, *The Mission of God*, 45-46.

Section 2

Chapter 4 — Look in Scripture

30. George W. Braswell Jr. *What You Need to Know About Islam and Muslims*. (Nashville: B&H, 2000), 10.
31. Reza Aslan. *No god but God*. (New York: Random House, 2011), 36.
32. Braswell Jr., *Islam and Muslims*, 10.
33. Braswell Jr., 10.
34. John Esposito. *What Everyone Needs to Know About Islam*. (Oxford University Press, 2011), 6.
35. Kenneth Mathews. *Genesis 11:27-50:26: The New American Commentary*. (Nashville: B&H, 2005), 190.
36. Mathews, *New American Commentary*, 190.
37. Victor P. Hamilton. *The Book of Genesis Chapters 1-17: The New International Commentary on the Old Testament*. (Grand Rapids, 1990), 446.
38. Kenneth Mathews, 190.
39. Reza Aslan. *No god but God*. (New York: Random House, 2011), 5.

40. Paige Patterson. *Revelation: The New American Commentary.* (Nashville: B&H, 2012), 200.

Chapter 5 — Look at the Path to Water
41. V. Gilbert Beers. *The Victor Handbook of Biblical Knowledge.* (Wheaton, IL: Victor Books, 1981), 355.
42. Andreas J. Kostenberger. *John: Baker Exegetical Commentary on the New Testament.* (Grand Rapids: Baker, 2008), 149.
43. D.A. Carson. *The Gospel of John: The Pillar New Testament Commentary.* (Grand Rapids: Eerdmans, 1991), 216.
44. Christopher Wright. *The Mission of God.* (Downers Grove, IL: InterVarsity, 2006), 200.
45. J. Ramsey Michaels. *John: New International Biblical Commentary.* (Peabody, MA: Hendrickson, 1989), 69.
46. Nabeel Qureshi. *Answering Jihad.* (Grand Rapids: Zondervan, 2016), 57.

Chapter 6 — Look to Nineveh
47. Leslie C. Allen. *The Books of Joel, Obadiah, Jonah, and Micah: The New International Commentary on the Old Testament.* (Grand Rapids: Eerdmans, 1976), 189.
48. Douglass Stewart. *Hosea-Jonah: Word Biblical Commentary.* (Grand Rapids: Zondervan, 1988), 464.
49. Andrew E. Hill and John H. Walton. *A Survey of the Old Testament.* (Grand Rapids: Zondervan, 1991), 496.
50. Allen, *New International Commentary,* 223.
51. Allen, 204-205.
0

Chapter 7 — Look to the Unclean
52. Nabeel Qureshi. *Seeking Allah, Finding Jesus.* (Grand Rapids: Zondervan, 2014), 65.
53. Kevin Greeson. *Camel Training Manual.* (Bangalore, India:

WIGTake Resources, 2004), 99.
54. Darrell Bock. *Acts: Baker Exegetical Commentary on the New Testament.* (Grand Rapids: Baker, 2007), 389.
55. Bock, *Baker Exegetical Commentary*, 389.
56. David Peterson. *The Acts of the Apostles: The Pillar New Testament Commentary.* (Grand Rapids: Eerdmans, 2009), 327.

Chapter 8 — Look Beyond the Wall of Partition
57. Thom and Jess Rainer. *The Millennials.* (Nashville: B&H, 2011).

Section 3

Chapter 12 — Look to the Future
58. Soren Kierkegaard. Soren Kierkegaard Research Center. (Copenhagen 1997, Volume 18), 306.
59. Andy Stanley. *Deep and Wide.* (Grand Rapids: Zondervan, 2012).

www.ingramcontent.com/pod-product-compliance
Lightning Source LLC
LaVergne TN
LVHW051657080426
835511LV00017B/2609